Essentials

of **Psychological Assessment** Series
Everything you need to know to administer, score, and interpret the major psychological tests.

I'd like to order the following *Essentials of Psychological Assessment*:

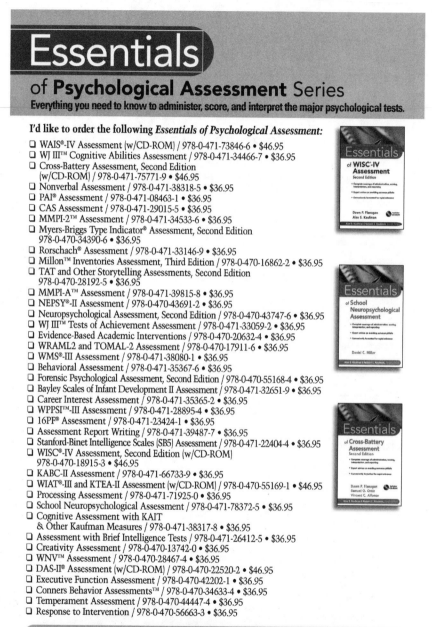

- ❏ WAIS®-IV Assessment (w/CD-ROM) / 978-0-471-73846-6 • $46.95
- ❏ WJ III™ Cognitive Abilities Assessment / 978-0-471-34466-7 • $36.95
- ❏ Cross-Battery Assessment, Second Edition
  (w/CD-ROM) / 978-0-471-75771-9 • $46.95
- ❏ Nonverbal Assessment / 978-0-471-38318-5 • $36.95
- ❏ PAI® Assessment / 978-0-471-08463-1 • $36.95
- ❏ CAS Assessment / 978-0-471-29015-5 • $36.95
- ❏ MMPI-2™ Assessment / 978-0-471-34533-6 • $36.95
- ❏ Myers-Briggs Type Indicator® Assessment, Second Edition
  978-0-470-34390-6 • $36.95
- ❏ Rorschach® Assessment / 978-0-471-33146-9 • $36.95
- ❏ Millon™ Inventories Assessment, Third Edition / 978-0-470-16862-2 • $36.95
- ❏ TAT and Other Storytelling Assessments, Second Edition
  978-0-470-28192-5 • $36.95
- ❏ MMPI-A™ Assessment / 978-0-471-39815-8 • $36.95
- ❏ NEPSY®-II Assessment / 978-0-470-43691-2 • $36.95
- ❏ Neuropsychological Assessment, Second Edition / 978-0-470-43747-6 • $36.95
- ❏ WJ III™ Tests of Achievement Assessment / 978-0-471-33059-2 • $36.95
- ❏ Evidence-Based Academic Interventions / 978-0-470-20632-4 • $36.95
- ❏ WRAML2 and TOMAL-2 Assessment / 978-0-470-17911-6 • $36.95
- ❏ WMS®-III Assessment / 978-0-471-38080-1 • $36.95
- ❏ Behavioral Assessment / 978-0-471-35367-6 • $36.95
- ❏ Forensic Psychological Assessment, Second Edition / 978-0-470-55168-4 • $36.95
- ❏ Bayley Scales of Infant Development II Assessment / 978-0-471-32651-9 • $36.95
- ❏ Career Interest Assessment / 978-0-471-35365-2 • $36.95
- ❏ WPPSI™-III Assessment / 978-0-471-28895-4 • $36.95
- ❏ 16PF® Assessment / 978-0-471-23424-1 • $36.95
- ❏ Assessment Report Writing / 978-0-471-39487-7 • $36.95
- ❏ Stanford-Binet Intelligence Scales (SB5) Assessment / 978-0-471-22404-4 • $36.95
- ❏ WISC®-IV Assessment, Second Edition (w/CD-ROM)
  978-0-470-18915-3 • $46.95
- ❏ KABC-II Assessment / 978-0-471-66733-9 • $36.95
- ❏ WIAT®-III and KTEA-II Assessment (w/CD-ROM) / 978-0-470-55169-1 • $46.95
- ❏ Processing Assessment / 978-0-471-71925-0 • $36.95
- ❏ School Neuropsychological Assessment / 978-0-471-78372-5 • $36.95
- ❏ Cognitive Assessment with KAIT
  & Other Kaufman Measures / 978-0-471-38317-8 • $36.95
- ❏ Assessment with Brief Intelligence Tests / 978-0-471-26412-5 • $36.95
- ❏ Creativity Assessment / 978-0-470-13742-0 • $36.95
- ❏ WNV™ Assessment / 978-0-470-28467-4 • $36.95
- ❏ DAS-II® Assessment (w/CD-ROM) / 978-0-470-22520-2 • $46.95
- ❏ Executive Function Assessment / 978-0-470-42202-1 • $36.95
- ❏ Conners Behavior Assessments™ / 978-0-470-34633-4 • $36.95
- ❏ Temperament Assessment / 978-0-470-44447-4 • $36.95
- ❏ Response to Intervention / 978-0-470-56663-3 • $36.95

Please complete the order form on the back.
To order by phone, call toll free 1-877-762-2974
To order online: www.wiley.com/essentials
To order by mail: refer to order form on next page

Essentials
of **Psychological Assessment** Series

ORDER FORM

Please send this order form with your payment (credit card or check) to:
John Wiley & Sons, Attn: J. Knott, 111 River Street, Hoboken, NJ 07030-5774

QUANTITY	TITLE	ISBN	PRICE

Shipping Charges:	Surface	2-Day	1-Day
First item	$5.00	$10.50	$17.50
Each additional item	$3.00	$3.00	$4.00
For orders greater than 15 items, please contact Customer Care at 1-877-762-2974.			

ORDER AMOUNT _____
SHIPPING CHARGES _____
SALES TAX _____
TOTAL ENCLOSED _____

NAME_____

AFFILIATION_____

ADDRESS_____

CITY/STATE/ZIP _____

TELEPHONE _____

EMAIL_____

❑ Please add me to your e-mailing list

PAYMENT METHOD:

❑ Check/Money Order ❑ Visa ❑ Mastercard ❑ AmEx

Card Number _____ Exp. Date _____

Cardholder Name *(Please print)* _____

Signature _____

*Make checks payable to **John Wiley & Sons**. Credit card orders invalid if not signed.*
All orders subject to credit approval. • Prices subject to change.

To order by phone, call toll free 1-877-762-2974
To order online: www.wiley.com/essentials

Ⓦ**WILEY**

Essentials of
Response to Intervention

Essentials of Psychological Assessment Series

Series Editors, Alan S. Kaufman and Nadeen L. Kaufman

Essentials

of Response to Intervention

Amanda M. VanDerHeyden
Matthew K. Burns

 John Wiley & Sons, Inc.

WILEY

Library of Congress Cataloging-in-Publication Data
VanDerHeyden, Amanda Mathany.
  Essentials of response to intervention/Amanda VanDerHeyden, Matthew K. Burns.
    p. cm.—(Essentials of psychological assessment series)
  Includes bibliographical references and index.
  ISBN 978-0-470-56663-3 (pbk.)
  1. Educational evaluation—United States. 2. Psychological tests for children—United States.
  3. Educational tests and measurement—United States. I. Burns, Matthew K. II. Title.
  LB2822.75.V373 2010
  379.1'58—dc22

                                                                    2009038787

Printed in the United States of America

10 9 8 7 6 5 4 3 2 1

We dedicate this book to the countless children with whom we have worked over the years and their teachers whose instructional efforts were reinforced by their student's successful learning.

Asa Hilliard wrote:

The risk for our children in school is not a risk associated with their intelligence. Our failures have nothing to do with IQ, nothing to do with race, nothing to do with language, nothing to do with style, nothing to do with the development of unique and differentiated special pedagogies, nothing to do with the children's families. All of these are red herrings. The study of them may ultimately lead to some greater insight into the instructional process, but at present, they serve to distract attention from the fundamental problem facing us today. We have one and only one problem: Do we truly will to see each and every child in this nation develop to the peak of his or her capacities? (p. 36, 1991).

We have been privileged to work with those who do have this will. Dr. VanDerHeyden would like to thank her best teachers: John Carruth, Calvin Baker, Laurie Emery, and Debbie Hedgepeth of Vail Unified School District, Joe Witt, Pat Snyder, and Chad, Ben, and Kate VanDerHeyden. Dr. Burns thanks James Tucker for teaching him; Katie Haegele, Becky Limm, David Parker, Shawna Peterson, and Sarah Scholin for learning with him; the staffs at Newport, Skyview, Park, and West Elementary Schools for letting him work in their buildings; and Mary Beth, Matthew, and Kate Burns for inspiring him.

Hilliard, A. (1991). Do we have the will to educate all children? *Educational Leadership*, *49*, 31–36.

CONTENTS

FOREWORD

I n the "old days," we called it diagnostic-prescriptive teaching. It evolved to diagnostic teaching, problem solving, intervention assistance, and eventually response to intervention (RtI). In the most recent rendition of Individuals with Disabilities Education Act (IDEA, 2004), RtI became legitimized as an alternative to the discrepancy model in identification of students with learning disabilities. So, what is this thing? Let's take a look at the multiple origins of RtI and at the multiple ways in which it is envisioned as a way of setting the stage for learning about the essentials of RtI.

Initially, diagnostic-prescriptive teaching involved administering tests and prescribing instructional interventions based on student performance on those tests. Although professionals did so in many ways, a major thrust was conducting profile analyses of student performance on one or more tests and designing instruction to maximize strengths and remediate or compensate for weaknesses. Professionals sought aptitude by treatment interactions and "diagnostic rules" for teaching specific types (or subtypes) of learners. As the diagnostic rules fell apart—that is, they did not work with much reliability—the use of tests in the diagnostic decision-making practice diminished, and people talked more about "diagnostic teaching." The general idea was that one could use data on actual student performance during instruction to answer the question (phrased here in Minnesotan language) "So how's it going there then?" for individual students. Sometimes the question was about progress toward short-term goals; at other times, it was toward general outcomes. Parents and teachers argued that they had a right and a need to know the extent to which students were profiting from their schooling experiences, and teachers specifically argued that they needed diagnostic information that would maximally inform instruction. And, teachers argued, the information provided by annual standardized tests was too little and too late.

In the mid-1960s, Samuel Kirk coined the term "learning disabled" (LD) to describe a group of students whose performance in school consistently was lower than we would expect based on assessments of their intelligence or learning aptitude. The condition was defined by a significant discrepancy between ability and academic achievement accompanied by deficits in one or more psychological processes (e.g., visual sequential memory) presumed important to success in school. It was thought that the way to develop appropriate and effective instruction for these students was to engage in diagnostic-prescriptive teaching (lots of assessments of learning strengths and weaknesses along with major efforts to differentiate instruction). Concurrently, educational psychologists such as Cronbach and Snow first searched for and advocated identification of aptitude by treatment interactions and then documented major difficulties in so doing. My colleagues and I (Cartwright, Cartwright, & Ysseldyke, 1973; Ysseldyke & Sabatino, 1973) made efforts to refine diagnostic-prescriptive models. In 1973, I wrote what turned out to be a seminal chapter (Ysseldyke, 1973) on the failure of the diagnostic-prescriptive model and the failure to reliably identify aptitude by treatment interactions, especially for students labeled as learning disabled. Arter and Jenkins (1979) similarly wrote a seminal article on the failure of the diagnostic-prescriptive model. Efforts to engage in diagnostic-prescriptive teaching based on correlates of academic difficulties diminished, as chronicled by Cronbach (1957) in his important *American Psychologist* article "The Two Disciplines of Scientific Psychology," in which he describes the shift in thinking from correlational to experimental psychology in the identification of appropriate treatments. Reschly and Ysseldyke (2002) described the ways in which there was a shift in paradigm in our diagnostic thinking and reported how this led to increased focus in assessment on problem solving and problem analysis.

So what's all this got to do with RtI and a book on the essentials of RtI? RtI is all about data-driven decision making. "While many definitions of RtI are offered, the process involves assignment of evidence-based instruction or interventions, monitoring of student progress, and the making of instructional or eligibility decisions based on progress-monitoring data" (Ysseldyke, 2008, p. 3). Elsewhere I have argued that RtI has its roots in the work on diagnostic teaching, and specifically in Ogden Lindsley's (1972) work on precision teaching. It also has as its origin a negative reaction to the use of ability measures and other process tests to diagnose and then remediate within-student deficits, dysfunctions, disorders, and disabilities. We (Ysseldyke & Salvia, 1974) described two models of diagnostic-prescriptive teaching, one based on attempts to remediate underlying ability deficits and the other based on identification and correction of deficits in skill development. It was argued that there was little evidence that test-named ability deficits existed, could be reliably and validly measured, and could be trained. Most important, we argued that process training would not transfer to improved educational outcomes for students. Rather a preferred model was advocated in which focus was on assessment of skill development strengths and weaknesses and direct instruction in academic skills.

Likely the first RtI project in the schools was the Sacajawea project in the Great Falls, Montana, Schools in the 1970's. Ray Beck and his colleagues implemented the precision teaching model developed by Lindsley, and teachers were trained to monitor progress toward short-term goals. At about the same time, in their classic text, *Data Based Program Modification*, Deno and Mirkin (1977) argued that there was no way to decide a priori the best way to teach a student. Rather, they contended that the best way to make instructional decisions was to teach, gather data on the extent to which alternative approaches worked, and then implement those approaches that worked best. At the Minnesota Institute for Research on Learning Disabilities, there were two lines of research. The first line of research focused on examining the extent to which there were reliable psychometric differences between students labeled LD and those who were assigned other labels (emotionally disturbed, low achieving). The other line of research focused on development of short, reliable, simple-to-administer measures of student progress within the classroom curriculum. Deno labeled these curriculum-based measures (CBMs). Results of that research are summarized in 144 research reports and additional papers in professional journals. In general, the researchers failed to identify technically adequate ways to differentiate categories of students, and they developed technically adequate CBMs. Concurrently, a group of administrators and researchers in Pennsylvania (Jim Tucker, Ed Gickling, and Joe Kovaleski) developed an instructional support team model that involved instructional consultation, problem solving, and the use of curriculum-based assessments.

Early work on CBM eventually led to the development of aimsweb, DIBELS, the Basic Skills Monitoring System, Individual Growth and Development Indicators, Easy CBM, Accelerated Math, and Yearly Progress Pro progress monitoring systems so prevalent today in RtI. CBM was also an important ingredient in the work of Dan Reschly, David Tilly, and Jeff Grimes on the Iowa Problem Solving Model, Andrea Canter and Doug Marston on the Minneapolis Public Schools Problem Solving Model, the Pennsylvania Instructional Support Teams (IST) model, the Screening to Enhance

Educational Progress (STEEP) model developed by Joe Witt and Amanda VanDerHeyden, and the work of Cathy Telzrow and her colleagues on the Ohio Intervention Based Assessments Team model.

Thus, RtI has its origins in resistance to the use of tests to identify ways to teach students experiencing difficulty and in the alternative of gathering data on actual student performance and using those data to plan, adapt, or modify instruction. It involves, as I noted, the use of data to make decisions about whether general education instruction is working (what I like to call monitoring response to instruction) or whether specifically designed interventions are working (what I like to call response to intervention).

RtI has taken many forms, some good and some not so good. Many things go on under the label of RtI, and it is critical that school personnel understand the essentials of good practice. In this text, Amanda VanDerHeyden and Matthew Burns provide a complete description of the essentials of RtI. Readers are provided an opportunity to learn directly from folks who have been in leadership roles on the front lines of the RtI effort. To what extent will RtI practices be sustained? The devil is in the details. First, it will be sustained if it lessens rather than increases instructional management activities for teachers. Second, it will be sustained if it is understood and implemented with intervention integrity (as so few educational practices are). To even get to these first two necessary matters, practitioners must understand the essentials of RtI, talk a common language, and know what it is they are talking about. It is the purpose of this text to provide that first step.

Jim Ysseldyke
Minneapolis, MN
August 28, 2009

REFERENCES

Arter, J. A., & Jenkins, J. A. (1979). Differential diagnosis-prescriptive teaching: A critical appraisal. *Review of Educational Research, 49,* 517–555.

Cartwright, G. P., Cartwright, C. A., & Ysseldyke, J. E. (1973). Two decision models: Identification and diagnostic teaching of handicapped children in the regular classroom. *Psychology in the Schools, 10,* 4–11.

Cronbach, L. (1957). The two disciplines of scientific psychology. *American Psychologist, 12,* 671–684.

Deno, S. I., & Mirkin, P. K. (1977). *Data-based program modification: A manual.* Minneapolis, MN: University of Minnesota Leadership Training Institute/Special Education.

Lindsley, O. R. (1972). From Skinner to precision teaching: The child knows best. In J. B. Jordan & L. S. Robbins (Eds.), *Let's try doing something else kind of thing* (pp. 1–11). Arlington, VA: Council for Exceptional Children.

Reschly, D. J., & Ysseldyke, J. E. (2002). Paradigm shift: The past is not the future. In A. Thomas & J. Grimes (Eds). *Best practices in school psychology IV*. Bethesda, MD: National Association of School Psychologists.

Salvia, J. A., Ysseldyke, J. E. & Bolt, S. E. (2010). *Assessment in special and inclusive education* (11th ed.) Boston: Cengage.

Ysseldyke, J. E. (1973). Diagnostic-prescriptive teaching: The search for aptitude x treatment interactions. In L. Mann & D. Sabatino (Eds.). *The first review of special education*. New York: Grune & Stratton.

Ysseldyke, J. E. (2008). *Frequently asked questions about response to intervention (RtI)*. Wisconsin Rapids, WI: Renaissance Learning.

Ysseldyke, J. E., & Sabatino, D. A. (1973). Toward validation of the diagnostic-prescriptive model. *Academic Therapy*, *8*, 415–422.

Ysseldyke, J. E., & Salvia, J. (1974). Diagnostic-prescriptive teaching: Two models. *Exceptional Children*, *41*, 181–186.

SERIES PREFACE

In the *Essentials of Psychological Assessment* series, we have attempted to provide the reader with books that will deliver key practical information in the most efficient and accessible style. The series features instruments in a variety of domains, such as cognition, personality, education, and neuropsychology. For the experienced clinician, books in the series will offer a concise yet thorough way to master utilization of the continuously evolving supply of new and revised instruments as well as a convenient method for keeping up to date on the tried-and-true measures. The novice will find here a prioritized assembly of all the information and techniques that must be at one's fingertips to begin the complicated process of individual psychological diagnosis.

Wherever feasible, visual shortcuts to highlight key points are utilized alongside systematic, step-by-step guidelines. Chapters are focused and succinct. Topics are targeted for an easy understanding of the essentials of administration, scoring, interpretation, and clinical application. Theory and research are continually woven into the fabric of each book, but always to enhance clinical inference, never to sidetrack or overwhelm. We have long been advocates of "intelligent" testing—the notion that a profile of test scores is meaningless unless it is brought to life by the clinical observations and astute detective work of knowledgeable examiners. Test profiles must be used to make a difference in the child's or adult's life, or why bother to test? We want this series to help our readers become the best intelligent testers they can be.

In *Essentials of RtI Assessment*, VanDerHeyden and Burns provide a cutting-edge text on a topic that is front and center for anyone involved in the assessment of children with specific learning disabilities. These authors, along with Ysseldyke who wrote the authoritative Foreword to the book, are true leaders in the field and are directly on the firing line. The book is a scholarly, research-based, "essential" book about RtI and its assessment that does much more than meet the authors primary hopes of facilitating effective implementation of RtI and preventing its misuse. The book provides hands-on practices and procedures for conducting effective response to intervention at every stage of the diagnostic and assessment process. Whereas we disagree emphatically with the authors' belief that cognitive assessment has little or no value in the diagnosis of SLD, we do believe that in-depth knowledge of the methodology and conceptual foundations of RtI assessment are crucial for all psychologists and educators. This book provides that knowledge and is a key part of our series.

Alan S. Kaufman, PhD, and Nadeen L. Kaufman, EdD, Series Editors
Yale University School of Medicine

VOLUME PREFACE

W hen we were young professionals beginning our careers, we witnessed first-hand the harm caused to students and families under the traditional eligibility determination process in schools. We watched young students struggle and systems fail to find ways to help these students who were often disproportionately poor and of minority ethnicity. We watched the eligibility process unfold like a series of hurdles filled with drama and tension for parents, students, teachers, and administrators and wondered at the futility of the process given that specialized help was unlikely to follow that would make a meaningful or measurable difference for the child. We saw children referred in high-achieving schools and made eligible for special education when that child may have gone to a different school in the same district and been the highest-achieving student in his class. We remember the names and faces of the young children with whom we worked doing very simple interventions that we had read about in articles that were 20-30 years old, using intervention strategies like modeling and guided practice and reinforcement of correct responses. We marveled when those strategies worked. We rejoiced when they worked for most of the most challenging children. We were puzzled and dismayed that children were failing when rather simple interventions often seemed to solve their problems. We remembered the values that brought us to our field: the desire for all students to learn, efficient and responsible resource allocation to support student learning, and the idea of a great public education being central to social justice and equity.

Shortly into our careers, we worked with productive and supportive mentors and quickly found a network of like-minded leaders who supported our work as we grew professionally. Through research and grassroots field implementations, the framework of RtI emerged before our eyes. We were honored to contribute to that knowledge base in a small way because we recognized that the moment was pivotal for education. Thus, we wrote this book for front-line implementers. We wrote this book for teachers who we admire each and every day and in the most basic sense wish to be of help to them in attaining better results for students. We also wrote this book for diagnosticians who often play an unforgettable role in the lives of students and their families, but who may be unaware of what constitutes technically adequate RtI implementation and may be using ineffective and invalidated practices (e.g., discrepancy-based identification of SLD).

We have two hopes for this book. The first is that it will facilitate effective implementation of RtI. The second hope is that it will prevent its misuse. We sincerely hope that the legacy of poorly implementing practices and then abandoning them for the next great idea will not occur with RtI, but we recognize this vulnerability. We have seen first-hand what RtI can do for systems and children. We believe all children deserve the best public education possible. We believe that every student, regardless of how he or she performed yesterday, can beat that score today with the right support. We know that RtI is transformational for schools that are struggling and we recognize like any innovation, it requires leadership to stay the course. We believe that RtI is an inevitable evolution of practice and a milestone for our science as opposed to some radical endpoint. We hope the science will grow and the practices will become more fine-tuned producing better results for our students and the families who entrust their education to us.

Amanda M. VanDerHeyden   Matthew K. Burns

One

OVERVIEW OF RESPONSE TO INTERVENTION

For decades the role of educational assessment in the United States has contradicted the very basis upon which education in this country was founded. Data collected by school psychologists and educational diagnosticians for the past 50 years were used to classify students as extremely high and low in order to rank them (Reschly, 1996). As Reynolds (1975) stated, "The dominant orientation in measurements was to a simple kind of prediction that supported the selection of high and rejection of low achievers" (p. 5). However, as early as 1749, Benjamin Franklin wrote in the *Proposals relating to the education of youth in Pennsylvania* that "*all* should be taught to write a fair hand, and swift, as that is useful to all" (Cutler, 1905, p. 56, emphasis added), and the founders clearly saw education as a means to ensure that all citizens could participate in business, express ideas, and fully involve themselves in a democracy (Rothstein & Jacobsen, 2006).

More recently, the Goals 2000 (1994) and No Child Left Behind (2001) legislations continued the line of federal regulations that emphasized the need for all students in this country to be proficient in the basic skills, and the dominant paradigm simultaneously changed from assessment *of* learning to assessment *for* learning (Stiggins, 2005). Assessment in the 1970s and 1980s focused on identifying aptitudes and cognitive processes that were linked to particular disabilities and to learning profiles that could be used to modify instruction. However, decades of research did not support that instructional modifications based on aptitude data led to improved or more robust student learning (Kavale & Forness, 1999). Thus, the U.S. Department of Education's Office of Special Education Programs recommended that measures of aptitude and cognitive processing *not* be used when identifying a child with a specific learning disability (SLD) asserting there is "no current evidence that such assessments are necessary or sufficient for identifying SLD" (*Federal Register*, 2006, p. 46651). Instead, school districts are now allowed to use a process to determine if a child responds to research-based interventions as part of the SLD identification evaluation. This process, commonly referred to as response to intervention (RtI), is quickly being adopted by school districts all across the country.

There are RtI implementation sites in all 50 states, but what constitutes RtI can be a matter of some debate. In education, there is a long history of widely adopting an innovation without first evaluating its research base or ensuring consistent implementation. When this happens, the innovation that was once hailed as the newest best practice often ends even more abruptly than it began, and "today's flagship" becomes "tomorrow's abandoned shipwreck" (Ellis, 2005, p. 200).

Because a solid research base and consistent implementation are both necessary components of an effective educational innovation (Ellis, 2005), this book will provide the details of both pertaining to RtI. Detailed in the pages that follow is a critique of old models of SLD diagnosis and a summary of the research base for RtI. Chapter 2 provides specific implementation guidelines. RtI is primarily the use of assessment data to make instructional and resource allocation decisions (Batsche et al., 2005; Burns & VanDerHeyden, 2006; Tilly 2008), one of which may be whether to identify a child as having a SLD. Thus, RtI is an assessment process with diagnostic implications. The purpose of this book is to specify characteristics of technically adequate RtI implementations such that accurate diagnostic decisions may be based on the results. A technical adequacy model is necessary to ensure that implementations contain the features that will result in desired implementation outcomes and to aid in the evaluation of implementation efforts in research and practice.

EMPIRICAL ROOTS OF RTI

Problems with the Old System

As stated, the federal provision for RtI came out of special education regulations. Special education was defined by the most recent Individuals with Disabilities Education Improvement Act (2004), as "specially designed instruction, at no cost to the parents or guardians, to meet the unique needs of a child with a disability" (§§ 300.39). Thus, special education relies on two facets: (a) providing effective instruction that is individualized to student needs, and (b) the valid identification of student disabilities. These two facets are highly related because valid diagnostic paradigms are those in which the data lead to interventions with known outcomes (Cromwell, Blashfield, & Strauss, 1975; Hayes, Nelson, & Jarrett, 1987; Messick, 1995). In other words, the diagnosis should lead to treatments with predictably positive outcomes, and failure to link the two results in a diagnostic framework that is fraught with invalid decisions. As discussed later, special education has a history of difficulties with both of its basic facets. Because RtI currently is allowed in federal SLD regulations, we focus our discussion on SLD.

Specially Designed Instruction

The first aspect of an effective approach to special education is individually designed instruction to provide educational benefit to individual students (*Hendrick Hudson School Board of Education v. Rowley*, 1982). However, previous research found no differences in the instruction delivered to students in special education classrooms as compared to students with and without disabilities in general education courses, or among students in the same special education class (Ysseldyke, O'Sullivan, Thurlow, & Christenson, 1989). Moreover, Glass's (1983) seminal meta-analysis found negative effects for academic and social outcomes for children in special education and concluded that "special placements continue to be made for reasons other than benefits to pupils" (p. 69).

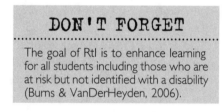

DON'T FORGET

The goal of RtI is to enhance learning for all students including those who are at risk but not identified with a disability (Burns & VanDerHeyden, 2006).

Concern about the effectiveness of special education was certainly an impetus to the RtI provision, but the goal of RtI is to enhance learning for all students including those who are at risk but not identified with a disability (Burns & VanDerHeyden, 2006). Special education used to operate very much like a bounty hunter system where increasing eligibility rates brought more money to a school. However, more recent iterations of the special education mandate allowed for funding to be distributed based on total student population in an attempt to sever the tie between categorized disabilities and monetary contingencies. Recent research has also suggested the need for reform in general education. Generally speaking, less than one-third of students in the elementary grades scored within a proficient range on recent assessments from the National Assessment of Educational Progress in math (Manzo & Galley, 2003), reading (National Center for Educational Statistics 2005), and writing (U.S. Department of Education, 2002).

Identification of SLD

When the federal regulations for Public Law (PL) 94–142 (1977, the precursor to the Individuals with Disabilities in Education Act) were written, there was no agreed upon diagnostic approach for SLD. The *Illinois Test of Psycholinguistic Ability* (Kirk, McCarthy, & Kirk, 1961) was the most commonly used approach to diagnose SLD during the 1960s and early 1970s, but it quickly fell out of favor due to concerns about the psychometric adequacy of the data (Hammill & Larsen, 1974; Mann, 1971; Ysseldyke & Salvia, 1974). Thus, when SLD became institutionalized in the 1977 regulations for PL 94–142, there was no agreed upon diagnostic criteria and the now-infamous discrepancy model was included in the regulations as a compromise (Gresham et al., 2005).

Research in the 30 years since then has questioned the validity of the discrepancy model on the basis of discriminant validity (i.e., lack of differences between students identified as SLD and struggling readers; Stuebing et al., 2002), consequential validity (i.e., outcomes are not enhanced by diagnosis and services in special education; Algozzine & Ysseldyke, 1983), and social inequity (i.e., disproportionality of and rapidly growing incidence of SLD diagnosis; Ysseldyke, Algozzine, & Epps, 1983). In fact, some have argued against IQ testing as part of SLD identification because of a lack of instructional relevance (Gresham & Witt, 1997; Siegel, 1988) and inability to discriminate readers who require intervention and those who do not (Vellutino, Scanlon, & Lyon, 2000).

More recent data demonstrating the effect of intervention on brain development questions the need for SLD diagnosis and suggests the simplest and most efficient route is to focus on delivering intervention to young students who are struggling to learn. Simos and colleagues (2001) conducted neurological imaging studies and found pre-intervention brain patterns of children identified with SLD that were consistent with an SLD diagnosis (i.e., focusing on the right hemisphere of the brain as they read or no clear pattern). However, after an 8-week intervention, the left cerebral hemisphere showed activity when they read, which was a normalized pattern, and suggested that intervention can be effective in remediating significant learning difficulties.

CAUTION

Research has prompted serious concerns about the validity of the discrepancy model on the basis of discriminant validity (i.e., lack of differences between students identified as SLD and struggling readers), consequential validity (i.e., outcomes are not enhanced by diagnosis and services in special education), and social inequity (i.e., disproportionality of and rapidly growing incidence of SLD diagnosis).

Some have suggested that the discrepancy model is not the best approach to diagnose SLD (Hale, Naglieri, Kaufman, & Kavale, 2004), and others argue that the construct of SLD is fundamentally flawed and will never be adequately conceptualized for identification purposes (Algozzine & Ysseldyke, 1982, Algozzine and Ysseldyke, 1983; Coles, 1998; Ysseldyke & Marston, 2000). Perhaps the only thing that can be stated with any confidence is that, once again, much like in 1977, there are no universally accepted diagnostic criteria for SLD.

POSITIVE FINDINGS OF EARLY RESEARCH

The consistent message from the positive effects of intervention research is that students with reading difficulties can learn at an acceptable rate with quality instruction and that SLD diagnosis can be prevented. Research consistently has demonstrated that instruction and intervention can prevent SLD diagnosis in later years (Lennon & Slesinski, 1999; Torgesen, Rose, Lindamood, Conway, & Garvan, 1999; Torgesen et al., 2001). For example, the seminal study by Foorman, Francis, and Fletcher (1998) compared three instructional strategies among 285 first- and second-grade students who were at risk for reading failure. They found that students who received direct instruction in letter sounds learned reading skills more quickly and had a lower rate of subsequent reading difficulties and SLD than those who were taught sound-symbol relationships by embedding them in connected text or those for whom this instruction was implicitly taught.

≋ Rapid Reference 1.1

Students who received direct instruction in letter sounds:
• Learned reading skills more quickly.
• Had a lower rate of subsequent reading difficulties and SLD.

In addition to preventing SLD diagnosis, effective intervention can lead to positive reading gains even among children with severe reading difficulties and disabilities (Lovett, Borden, Lacerenza, Benson, & Brackstone, 1994; McGuinness, McGuinness, & McGuinness, 1996; Wise, Ring, & Olson, 1999). Some of the components of effective interventions for children with severe reading difficulties include making decisions with formative evaluation (Fuchs & Fuchs, 1986), delivering instruction in small interactive groups (Vaughn, Gersten, & Chard, 2000), and various instructional components such as drill-repetition-practice-feedback, controlling task difficulty, and directed response/questioning

(Swanson, 1999). Moreover, meta-analytic research among students with SLD found large effects for several interventions including mnemonic strategies, explicit instruction, and instruction in comprehension strategies (Kavale & Forness, 1999).

Given the documented poor outcomes associated with special education particularly for children diagnosed with SLD, it seems that preventing learning difficulties is superior to treating them. Moreover, the long history of cultural biases in special education and SLD diagnostic practices (Donovan & Cross, 2002) suggested that alternatives were needed.

RTI DEFINITION AND PURPOSE

RtI is not a new concept (Fuchs & Fuchs, 1998; Velluntino et al., 1996), but it was included in federal legislation only recently, and there seems to be considerable confusion about its implementation (Fuchs, Mock, Morgan, & Young, 2003). The National Association of State Directors of Special Education defined RtI as the practice of providing high-quality instruction, changing instruction based on frequent progress monitoring, and making important educational decisions based on student response to the changed instruction/intervention (Batsche et al., 2005). Others have conceptualized RtI as the systematic use of data to most efficiently allocate resources to enhance outcomes for all students (Burns & VanDerHeyden, 2006). Thus, the commonly described components of RtI are: (a) quality core instruction; (b) universal screening; (c) progress monitoring for students identified with difficulties; (d) increasingly intensive interventions implemented based on student need; and (e) resulting data used to make instructional, resource allocation, placement, and special education identification decisions.

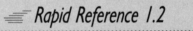

Rapid Reference 1.2

Components of RtI are:
• Quality core instruction
• Universal screening
• Progress monitoring for students identified with difficulties
• Increasingly intensive interventions implemented based on student need
• Resulting data used to make instructional, resource allocation, placement, and special education identification decisions

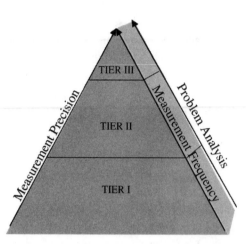

Figure 1.1 Measurement and Problem Analysis Within a Response to Intervention Model.

Source: Based on Burns & Gibbons (2008).

RtI models include multiple tiers of service delivery with most including three tiers. As displayed in Figure 1.1 (Burns & Gibbons, 2008), three things happen as students' needs become more intense and they progress through the tiers. Measurement becomes more frequent and precise, and problem analyses become more detailed and costly. Information about the three tiers on these three issues follows.

> **DON'T FORGET**
> ....
> It is better to prevent learning difficulties than to treat them, and early intervention shows potential to prevent learning difficulties that otherwise might lead to an SLD diagnosis.

Tier I

The first tier of any RtI model is quality core instruction. It would be beyond the scope of this book to discuss what constitutes quality reading and math instruction, but assessing the quality of core instruction is a prerequisite to any effective RtI model. Measurement in Tier 1 usually is based on general outcome measures (GOMs), which are essentially general assessments of a student's overall academic performance. For this reason, these assessments often are referred to as the vital signs of learning in that they can be used to reflect in a meaningful way whether children are at risk or not in their instructional programs. Measurement in an RtI system usually relies on general outcome measures referred to as curriculum-based measurements of reading (CBM-R) and math (CBM-M) because they are sensitive to growth and psychometrically adequate for most decisions (e.g., determining who is at risk, evaluating effects of instruction; National Center on Response to Intervention, 2009). However, Tier 1 assessments may be conducted with less sensitive, but highly reliable, group- or computer-administered tools, such as the Measures of Academic Progress (Northwest Evaluation Association, 2003), Star Math (Renaissance Learning, 1998), and Star Reading (Renaissance Learning, 2003). The goal of assessments within Tier 1 is that they adequately identify a student as proficient in required skills or as needing additional intervention and that they do so in the most efficient way possible (i.e., at the lowest cost to instructional time).

The assessments used in Tier 1 usually are conducted three times each year. Certainly some measures could be conducted more frequently as resources allow and as the data warrant. However, data collected as part of the school's resource allocation system probably should be collected no less than three times each academic year, usually within the first month of school, sometime in January, and again within the last month of the school year.

Because the data collected in Tier 1 are designed to inform a screening or risk decision and are collected somewhat infrequently, only low-level problem analyses are possible. Essentially, the two primary purposes for collecting data within Tier 1 are to (a) identify students who need additional intervention and (b) determine if the problem is specific to the student or the student's classroom. VanDerHeyden and colleagues (VanDerHeyden & Burns, 2005; VanDerHeyden, Witt, & Gilbertson, 2007; VanDerHeyden, Witt, & Naquin, 2003) have consistently demonstrated that class-wide interventions are more efficient and effective when a large portion of the students in one classroom or grade require intervention. In other words, sometimes it is more efficient to take the intervention to the classroom than it is to take students to an intervention. Moreover, quality core instruction is the basis from which all interventions occur. Interventions have a greater likelihood of success if they are highly (and correctly) targeted (Burns, VanDerHeyden, & Boice, 2008), but students learn the skill only if the intervention is contextualized in the broader curriculum. Take reading, for example. A struggling elementary-age reader probably would benefit from additional explicit instruction in sound-symbol relationships, but children cannot be taught how to read simply by learning how to sound out words. The intervention will work only if it is integrated with quality core instruction; without good teaching and curriculum, little else matters.

CAUTION

Class-wide interventions are an efficient and effective way to improve learning where many students are struggling. However, supplemental intervention will work only if it is integrated with quality core instruction. Without good teaching and curriculum, little else matters.

Tier 2

Where Tier 1 instruction is adequate, estimates suggest that up to 20% of students will not be successful despite quality core curriculum and instruction (Burns, Appleton, & Stehouwer, 2005). A Tier 2 intervention is implemented for children identified as struggling learners and for whom a class-wide intervention was either not needed or after it has improved the skills of most students in the classroom. Tier 2 interventions usually are delivered in small groups of 2 to 8 (5 being most common) in elementary school, approximately 8 to 10 for middle school grades, and 10 to 12 or even 15 with high school students. Students are flexibly and fluidly grouped in homogeneous groups based on baseline and progress monitoring data. For example, students who need additional instruction in sound-symbol relationships are in one group, those who need phonemic awareness instruction are in another, and fluency building groups could be in a third. Intervention sessions can be conducted effectively approximately 30 minutes each session 3 to 5 days per week.

Measurement at Tier 2 focuses on more detailed quantification of the learning or performance deficit. Whereas Tier 1 data are used to make a screening decision, Tier 2 data are needed to determine what prerequisite skills are missing and what instructional conditions might accelerate learning (e.g., Does the student demonstrate phonemic awareness? How well does she decode words? How fluent is her reading? and How well does she comprehend what she reads?). These data are used to create homogenous skill groups in order to match the intervention to student need. In addition to being more precise than Tier 1 data, Tier 2 data are collected more frequently. Assessments in Tier 1 occur three times each year, but data are collected in Tier 2 once each week or no less than once every other week. These more frequently collected data are used to monitor progress, to move children between groups, and to judge the effectiveness of the intervention.

Tier 3

On average, 2% to 5% of the student population will require intervention intensity beyond what is provided in Tier 2 (Burns et al., 2005). For those students, interventions are highly targeted, are developed based on individual student need, and are often delivered in 1-to-1 (1 child to 1 adult) or 2-to-1 formats. Thus, assessment data must go well beyond simply determining how proficient students are in the skill; they must also identify specific skills and skill components that the student knows and does not know. For example, a Tier 1 math assessment would identify a struggling math student and identify a class-wide problem; data collected in Tier 2 would identify automaticity of single-digit multiplication facts as the most appropriate intervention target; but Tier 3 assessments could determine if the student has conceptual knowledge of multiplication (e.g., can use multiplication to find a least common denominator) and which facts the individual student knows and does not know.

DON'T FORGET

Data at Tier 1 are used to make a screening decision. Data at Tier 2 are needed to:
- determine what prerequisite skills are missing and what instructional conditions might accelerate learning,
- monitor intervention progress,
- move children between groups, and
- judge the effectiveness of the intervention.

Data at Tier 3 are needed to:
- build an intervention that will accelerate learning if correctly implemented,
- monitor intervention progress,
- address and adjust integrity and intervention facets to ensure maximal effects, and
- evaluate the intervention effects.

Following the pattern of increased precision and frequency, data are collected in Tier 3 at least once each week to monitor progress. Progress monitoring data collected in Tiers 2 and 3 are often general outcome measures or CBMs (e.g., oral reading fluency and digits correct per minute on a multiskill math probe), but progress should also be monitored in the specific skill being taught (e.g., nonsense-word fluency for a phonics intervention or single-digit multiplication probes). However, even more precise data are used to determine the appropriate intervention and often take into account factors such as the accuracy with which a skill is completed and malleable environmental factors that could contribute to the problem, such as instruction, curriculum, learning environment, and learner characteristics (Hosp, 2008). Some have suggested testing various interventions to determine which is most successful for an individual student (Daly, Witt, Marens, & Dool, 1997) and using those data to build the intervention (Barnett, Daly, Jones, & Lentz, 2004). In other words, Tier 3 data should help identify the cause of poor academic performance. The purpose of assessment at Tier 3 is to identify an intervention that will accelerate learning when it is delivered before resources are dedicated to deploying that intervention in the classroom.

EARLY IMPLEMENTATION MODELS

Whereas the roots of RtI can be traced to multiple events and literatures, looking back, certain events were seminal for RtI. The University of Minnesota's Institute for Research on Learning Disabilities (IRLD) in the late 1970s greatly influenced the development of what later came to be called RtI. The IRLD conducted groundbreaking research on SLD diagnosis that systematically examined the foundations of SLD diagnosis and service delivery. Those studies caused earthquake effects to the basis and purpose of SLD diagnosis and created impetus for more direct services that would advance student outcomes. Deno and Mirkin's (1977) *Data-Based Program Modification* (DBPM) manual operationalized a problem-solving model for identifying and responding to student learning problems using brief timed measures (CBMs) to inform and evaluate instructional efforts. This important little manual organized and advanced the work of Bloom, Hastings, and Madaus (1971) and those in the precision teaching field, especially Starlin and Starlin (1973), and started the firestorm of research and development on curriculum-based or general outcome measurement. Deno and Mirkin (1977) operationalized a problem-solving process that became the basis for both early and contemporary implementation efforts in what later was referred to as RtI. In the measurement arena, visionary researchers were beginning to raise the idea of contextualized assessment and accurate decision making (Dawes, Faust, & Meehl, 1989) and promoting the idea of treatment utility and consequential validity as a basis for psychological measurement (Messick, 1995).

It is commonly said that we stand on the shoulder of giants, and it is true within RtI implementation as well. Although most implementation initiatives occurred within the past 5 years, a handful of districts and state agencies were engaged in RtI activities decades before RtI was included in federal regulations. Fuchs et al. (2003) identified four major models to which many of the current RtI models can be traced. Brief descriptions of the four models identified by Fuchs et al. are presented next.

The Heartland Area Educational Agency 11 (Heartland) implemented a four-level problem-solving model in 1985 (Ikeda & Gustafson, 2002). Levels I and II involved educational professionals consulting with the child's parents (Level I) and then the school's assistance team (BAT) (Level II). Intervention efforts in Levels I and II were implemented exclusively by school personnel; Heartland staff did not become involved until Level III, at which time teams worked with school personnel in an extended problem-solving process. Finally, students for whom intervention efforts in Level III were not successful were considered for special education eligibility (Level IV). Heartland recently transitioned to a three-tier model (Tilly, 2003) and remains one of the best-known and most well-respected RtI implementation sites in the country.

Minneapolis Public Schools (MPS) also implemented a problem-solving model (PSM) in 1993 that merged special and general education personnel (Marston, Muyskens, Lau, & Canter, 2003). The PSM closely monitored student progress, accommodated students in general education, and provided a non-biased method of identifying children in need of special education (MPS, 2001). There are three stages in the PSM that progress from teacher classroom interventions based on universal screenings (Stage 1), to refined interventions and progress-monitoring strategies developed by a problem-solving team (Stage 2), and consideration of special education referral in Stage 3 (Marston et al., 2003). Although school districts across the country only recently have begun using RtI data for eligibility decisions, MPS did so through a state waiver over 15 years ago and was among the first to do so.

Pennsylvania's Instructional Support Team (IST) model was phased into all elementary schools of the state's 501 school districts over a 5-year period that began in 1990 (Kovaleski, Tucker, & Duffy, 1995). The model was implemented in an attempt to bridge special and general education programs by shifting the focus of special education from categorical services to effective instruction in general education (Kovaleski et al., 1996). The primary component of the IST model was the instructional support teacher who was specially trained and who worked exclusively with classroom general education teachers to assist with struggling learners (Kovaleski et al., 1995). However, the instructional support teacher did not deliver direct support to any students beyond modeling instructional approaches for the classroom teacher and occasional short-term interventions. The instructional support teacher could provide support for 50 school days, at which time the IST met to discuss student progress and decide if the student would be referred for a multidisciplinary evaluation for special education eligibility.

There were no formal phases or stages within IST, but three basic steps were followed:

1. An initial consultation took place between the classroom teacher and a consulting member of the IST.
2. Teacher concerns were behaviorally defined and the IST was convened.
3. The IST developed interventions that were collaboratively implemented by the classroom teacher and the support teacher (Pawlowski, 2001). IST was described as "the best-known statewide pre-referral intervention program in the nation" (Fuchs et al., 2003, p. 162). In addition to Pennsylvania, it was implemented on much smaller scales in Connecticut, Michigan, New York, and Virginia.

Ohio's statewide Intervention-Based Assessment (IBA) model emphasized functional and direct assessments of academic difficulties to identify and evaluate interventions for student learning and behavioral difficulties (Barnett et al., 1999). The multidisciplinary team (MDT) consisted of educational professionals and the child's parents and relied heavily on conjoint behavioral consultation (Telzrow et al., 2000). There were no specific phases in IBA and no mandated timelines. However, the MDT could conduct a special education eligibility evaluation at any time in the process if instructional methods necessary for success represented specially designed instruction, the child's characteristics matched the federal definition of one or more special education disabilities, and it was determined that the condition would have had an adverse effect on the child's education without special education and related services (McNamara & Hollinger, 2003). Much like IST, IBA was essentially a prereferral intervention process.

CURRENT PRACTICE AND RESEARCH

RtI has moved from isolated islands to a widespread network with a continuum of implementation progress. As stated earlier, there are RtI implementation sites in all 50 states, but Jimerson, Burns, and VanDerHeyden (2007) identified six RtI models, in addition to the four aforementioned ones, that were a second-wave of implementation leaders. These leaders include the St. Croix River Education District in Minnesota; the Illinois Flexible Service Delivery model; the System to Enhance Educational Performance (STEEP) operating in districts in several states; Michigan's Integrated Behavior and Learning Support Initiative; Idaho's Results-Based Model; and Florida's Problem-Solving statewide model. Clearly the practice is widespread and growing.

Recent research supports the recent growth in RtI initiatives. Specifically, implementing an RtI model resulted in more children demonstrating proficient skills on state accountability tests (Heartland, 2004; Sornson, Frost, & Burns, 2005; VanDerHeyden & Burns, 2005), improved reading skills among children identified as at-risk for reading failure (Marston et al., 2003; Tilly, 2003), more accurate and equitable identification of students in need of special education (VanDerHeyden et al., 2003; VanDerHeyden & Witt, 2005), and fewer children being placed into special education (Burns et al., 2005; Sornson et al., 2005; VanDerHeyden et al., 2007). Approximately 5.7% of school-age children were identified with a SLD (United States Department of Education, 2002), but fewer than 2% of the student population in various studies and program evaluations of RtI were identified with SLD (Burns et al., 2005). Perhaps one of the most comprehensive and experimentally rigorous evaluations of a multitiered intervention model found that students increased reading achievement and the percentage of new placements in special education fell from 15% to 8% (O'Connor, Harty, & Fulmer, 2005). Moreover, children with identified disabilities in an RtI model received more services and additional specialized instruction as compared to more traditional approaches (Ikeda & Gustafson, 2002; Reschly & Starkweather, 1997), and special education services began at earlier grades (Reschly & Starkweather, 1997).

Schools and school districts have only recently begun moving RtI principles and procedures to middle and high schools, and research thus far has been scant. Vaughn et al. (in press) implemented a large-scale RtI initiative with seven middle schools and examined the effectiveness of a Tier 2 intervention. Those students who received the intervention outperformed the control group on several reading measures including word attack, comprehension, and phonemic decoding, but the effects were small. Implementation at the high school level is probably even rarer than middle school, but Burns (2008) describes a model that currently is used in practice, and previous efforts resulted in positive outcomes with reading scores of participating ninth-grade students growing at a rate three times that of typical students and more than five times greater than their own growth in eighth grade (Windram, Scierka, & Silberglitt, 2007). Although additional research is needed, there is an evidence base from which to build RtI implementation efforts.

SUMMARY

The movement toward RtI began in 1977 with the publication of the *Data-Based Program Modification* manual (Deno & Mirkin, 1977), and subsequent research has suggested positive effects. One of the key components of effective intervention is the use of formative evaluation (Fuchs & Fuchs, 1986) and assessment data to determine which interventions would have the highest likelihood of success (Burns et al., 2008). Thus, RtI again has emphasized the importance of assessment data within the instructional process (Gresham, 2002) and renewed the debate about what constitutes instructionally relevant assessment data (Batsche, Kavale, & Kovaleski, 2006; Gresham et al., 2004; Hale et al., 2004).

In our opinion, again returning to the wisdom of Reynolds (1975): "[In] today's context the measurement technologies ought to become integral parts of instruction designed to make a difference in the lives of children and not just a prediction about their lives" (p. 15). The vision for assessment written by Reynolds and Stiggins (2005) and others has not yet reached fruition for a number of reasons. However, RtI presents perhaps the best opportunity for educational assessment to reach its potential since 1905 when Alfred Binet translated his test into English. Positive outcomes have been found in early implementation, but only when specific implementation procedures, assessment practices, and decision rules were used.

TEST-YOURSELF QUESTIONS

1. Why does a system like RtI have diagnostic implications for students?
2. Historically, SLD identification practices have been criticized as having poor consequential validity. What is the basis for this criticism?
3. Define RtI. What are the key components needed for RtI implementation?
4. What decisions are made based on assessment data collected at Tier 1?
5. Does it make sense to implement Tier 2 intervention in the face of inadequate Tier 1 or core instructional practices?
6. What percentage of students may be expected to need Tier 2 intervention? What percentage of students may be expected to need Tier 3 intervention?
7. What research evidence suggests that RtI can be used to reach decisions that have consequential validity for students and systems?

Answers:
1. Because RtI use creates a data set that can be used to determine eligibility for services under the category of SLD.
2. There is no evidence that making the diagnosis leads to treatment that enhances outcomes. Traditionally there has been poor classification agreement and little basis for discriminating between those with poor academic skills and those with SLD.
3. RtI is a system of decision making to allocate instructional resources to enhance learning outcomes for all students. Components include quality core instruction, progress monitoring for students below criterion, increasingly intensive interventions implemented based on student need, and resulting data used to allocate resources and make special education eligibility decisions.

(continued)

4. Identification of system and individual learning problems (i.e., screening), evaluation of adequacy of core instruction.
5. No.
6. Up to 20% may need Tier 2 intervention; 5% to 10% may need Tier 3 intervention.
7. With properly implemented RtI, student learning improves and diagnosis even may be prevented.

Two

HOW TO IMPLEMENT RTI

Response to intervention (RtI) has the potential to improve the efficiency and accuracy of resource allocation decisions. However, the meaning of the decisions and their potential to advance student learning outcomes depends on the adequacy of the underlying data. Most educators are familiar with the tenets of classical test theory as a basis for understanding the value of a given test score. Whereas RtI shares some of the conventional standards for reliability and validity, it requires something more. RtI is not a single-point-in-time measurement or package of measurements. As shown in Figure 2.1, RtI is measurement followed by particular instructional manipulations, followed by correctly selected and implemented measurement in iterations until a final decision can be made. Hence, the validity of decisions made within RtI hinges on the validity of (1) instructional manipulations, (2) student performance measurement, and (3) accuracy of decisions reached at each data interpretation time point.

Universal screening data must be collected in order to implement RtI. These data will be used to identify students in a given population who may be expected to fail without some change to their instructional programs. Universal screening measures should be direct measures of student performance that are brief yet meaningfully forecast future student learning without some instructional change. The measures must be brief to minimize the cost to instructional time and to permit their use at routine intervals during the school year. The scores yielded must be stable across brief intervals of time where little instruction has occurred. Universal screening measures must reflect local expectations for student performance and yield scores that sensitively distinguish between those students who are at risk and those who are not at risk. Many commonly used educational assessment tools do not meet these basic requirements for universal screening.

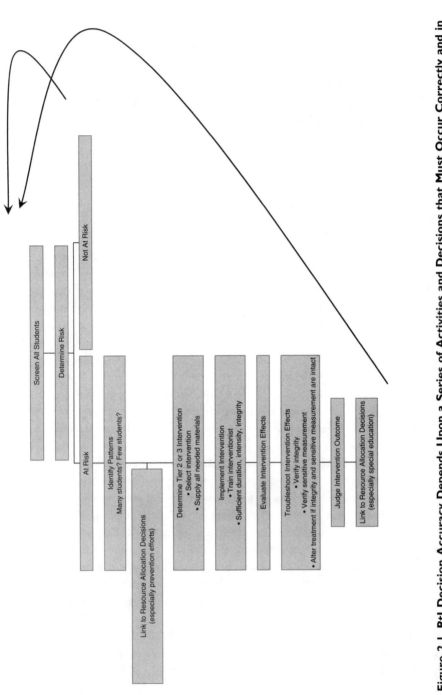

Figure 2.1 RtI Decision Accuracy Depends Upon a Series of Activities and Decisions that Must Occur Correctly and in Correct Sequence for the Decisions to have Validity.

≡ Rapid Reference 2.1

Universal screening measures should
- Be reliable.
- Be brief.
- Reflect future performance without intervention.
- Accurately and efficiently discriminate between students at risk and students not at risk.
- Be tied to local expectations for student learning.

It is worth noting that teacher identification has not been empirically supported as a viable universal screening tool (Marston, Mirkin, & Deno, 1984; Shinn, Tindal, & Spira, 1987; VanDerHeyden, Witt, & Naquin, 2003), even though teacher ratings typically are well correlated with students' rank-order based on some external criterion measure (Gerber & Semmel, 1984; Gerber, 2005). In fact, teacher referral accuracy is a perfect example of why a measure that is highly correlated with a criterion (in this case, teacher rankings of student performance and rankings based on some validated measure of student performance, such as curriculum-based measurement) is not necessarily a useful screening tool. Teacher rank-order may be stable, but the judgment about whether performance warrants referral for evaluation is highly variable across teachers and dependent on the local context. Teachers tend to identify students who do not need intervention at high rates (i.e., false positive identification errors) and also fail to identify those who do need intervention (i.e., false negative identification errors). The most frequently used screening tool in RtI is curriculum-based measurement (CBM). The technical characteristics of CBM scores make them ideal for use in RtI models. CBMs are brief, direct measures of student learning that have been shown to reliably indicate current levels of student performance and meaningfully forecast future performance without intervention. Further, CBMs have the advantage of being sensitive to student learning that occurs during instruction. Hence, CBMs are ideal universal screening measures.

OBTAINING AND INTERPRETING UNIVERSAL SCREENING DATA

The first stage of RtI involves screening all students in the school. Two decisions will be made with the scores obtained from universal screenings:

1. Is Tier 1 instruction (sometimes called "core" instruction) working for most students in the instructional setting?
2. Which students are in need of supplemental instruction to move out of the risk range of performance?

Selecting a Screening Task

The first step is to select the screening task. State-specified standards for student performance, available through state departments of education Web sites, are an excellent starting point for selecting universal screening tasks. For reading, CBM oral reading fluency and maze measures have been demonstrated to be useful and sensitive tools for universal screening (Jenkins, Hudson, & Johnson, 2007). For mathematics, computation probes that reflect key skills at each grade level can be readily identified using the state-specified performance standards. The appearance of particular mathematics computation skills and the order in which they appear in various standards does not vary greatly across states (Connell, Witt, Komatsu, Codding, & VanDerHeyden, in submission) and non–state-specific sequences for mathematics skills development and instruction (Shapiro, 2004). For writing, story starter sentence fragments can be used to obtain timed writing samples from students from grades 1 through 12. These writing samples can be scored in a variety of ways to indicate general writing proficiency using this 3-minute measure. Table 2.1 provides suggested screening measures for use at fall and spring in reading, mathematics, and writing from preK through 8th grade.

It is important to select a task difficulty level at screening that reflects an instructional level for the average student at that point in the school year. Functionally, this means that the screening measures a skill that has been taught and that the average student is expected to be able to do to benefit from the instruction that is to come at a given grade level. There may be a temptation to select an easier or more challenging task based on teacher and/or administrator perceptions about student capabilities. It is important to avoid this temptation and instead select a task tied to the local standards for performance at that time in the year that will allow users

DON'T FORGET

Two decisions will be made with the scores obtained from universal screenings:

- Is Tier 1 instruction (sometimes called "core" instruction) working for most students in the instructional setting?
- Which students are in need of supplemental instruction to move out of the risk range of performance?

Table 2.1 Suggested Screening Measures by Grade and Topic

	Math		Reading		Writing	
	Fall	Spring	Fall	Spring	Fall	Spring
Pre-K	• Counting objects aloud • Select a number (1–10) • Rapid discrimination	• Counting objects aloud • Rapid number naming	• Alliteration • Rhyming • Visual discrimination	• Rhyming • Alliteration • Letter names • Visual discrimination	• Visual discrimination	• Copying letters • Copying numbers • Writing name
Kindergarten	• Counting objects and selecting matching number (1–10) • Quantity discrimination • Rapid discrimination	• Counting objects and writing numbers (1–10)	• Phonemic awareness (e.g., phoneme segmentation fluency)	• Phonemic awareness	• Rapid discrimination • Copying letters	• Rapid discrimination • Copying letters
1st Grade	• Sums to 5	• Sums to 18 or 20	• Oral reading fluency (nonsense words, words, sentences, or passage)	• Oral reading fluency (passage)	• Copying letters • Story starter (scored for correct word sequences)	• Story starter (scored for correct word sequences)
2nd Grade	• Addition and subtraction 0–20	• Multidigit addition or subtraction without regrouping	• Oral reading fluency	• Oral reading fluency	• Story starter (scored for correct word sequences)	• Story starter (scored for correct word sequences)
3rd Grade	• Fact families Addition/subtraction 0–20 or three-digit addition and subtraction with and	• Multiplication 0–9 or 0–12	• Oral reading fluency	• Oral reading fluency	• Story starter (scored for correct word sequences)	• Story starter (scored for correct word sequences)

(continued)

Table 2.1 (continued)

	Math		Reading		Writing	
	Fall	Spring	Fall	Spring	Fall	Spring
	without regrouping (this is hard for most third graders but reflects a skill that most are expected to be able to do)					
4th Grade	• Fact families • Multiply/divide 0–12	• Multi-digit multiplication without or with regrouping	• Oral reading fluency	• Oral reading fluency	• Story starter (scored for correct word sequences)	• Story starter (scored for correct word sequences)
5th Grade	• Multi-digit multiplication with and without regrouping	• 1 digit into 2–3-digit dividend with remainders	• Oral reading fluency • Mazes	• Oral reading fluency • Mazes	• Story starter (scored for correct word sequences)	• Story starter (scored for correct word sequences)
6th Grade	• Decimals multiplication	• Find least common denominator	• Mazes	• Mazes	• Story starter (scored for correct word sequences)	• Story starter (scored for correct word sequences)
7th Grade	• Mixed operations for integers	• Mixed operations for fractions or percentages	• Mazes	• Mazes	• Story starter (scored for correct-incorrect word sequences)	• Story starter (scored for correct-incorrect word sequences)
8th Grade	• Mixed operations for fractions	• Solve simple algebraic proportions	• Mazes	• Mazes	• Story starter (scored for correct-incorrect word sequences)	• Story starter (scored for correct-incorrect word sequences)

to answer the first question about the adequacy of Tier 1 instruction. If the selected task results in a negatively skewed distribution (i.e., the task is challenging and many students do not demonstrate proficiency on the expected skill), then that outcome suggests a class-wide, grade-wide, or school-wide learning problem. Where many children are not proficient in skills that are expected and required for future learning, then the adequacy of Tier 1 instruction must be questioned. If the selected task results in a positively skewed distribution (i.e., the task is easy and many students demonstrate proficiency on the expected skill), then that outcome suggests that students as a whole are thriving in Tier 1 instruction and that instruction may even be accelerated or enriched.

CAUTION

Screening tasks should reflect a skill or skills that have been taught and that the average student is expected to be able to do to benefit from the instruction that is to come at a given grade level. Where skewed performance distributions are observed, additional assessment and possibly class-wide intervention will be necessary to reach accurate screening decisions: Are most students benefiting from core instruction? Which students are at risk?

When score distributions are skewed, it may be difficult to make between-student discriminations. That is, where many children perform poorly on the screening task, a floor effect may occur that will limit the ability to reach conclusions about risk status among the lower-performing students in the group (because their scores are similar). Where many children perform well on the screening task, a ceiling effect may occur. Whereas a ceiling effect may be less detrimental to reaching accurate screening decisions about which students are most at risk in a class (because scores are constrained for the higher-achieving students who are not at risk), if a benchmark criterion is used, children who are at risk may be missed because the task was simply too easy. For example, administering a third-grade-level reading passage to fifth-grade students would result in higher mean scores and probably provide a meaningful rank-order of students' general reading competence for a screening decision (permitting between-student comparisons in capability). However, it is highly likely that some of the students who should be considered at risk—that is, students who would not be able to read fifth-grade-level content—would successfully read third-grade-level content. Use of a too-easy task can result in false negative screening errors. Hence, where skewed distributions occur, a trial of controlled instruction is required before a second set of scores can be obtained to identify individual students in need of further intervention.

Grade-level teams of teachers can work together to select screening materials. Generally, this meeting is a useful opportunity for the grade-level teams to review expectations for learning in sequence across the grade level (reviewing state standards) and to identify essential skills that underlie further skill development. Providing teachers an opportunity to consider an array of screening tasks and identify the one that will work best in their classrooms enhances teacher buy-in and believability of the data and sets the occasion for a focus on instructional outcomes.

Accurate screening decisions can be made based on a single trial or single score of CBM. Historically it has been conventional to administer three timed CBM probes and calculate a median score during screening. Research has demonstrated, however, that three trials are not necessary to reach a screening decision (Ardoin et al., 2004; VanDerHeyden, Witt, & Naquin, 2003).

≡ Rapid Reference 2.2

- Using CBM, a single trial or single score is sufficient to reach a screening decision.
- Using a single score rather than three trials and a median score reduces total screening time by 67%.
- More extensive assessment can be undertaken for those found to be at risk during screening.

Administering the Screening Task

To obtain meaningful data, screening measures must be administered correctly. Standardized procedures should be followed to obtain meaningful scores. One way to accomplish efficient and accurate screening is to screen an entire school on the same day. Grade levels can be scheduled in 1-hour rolling blocks. Figure 2.2 shows a sample screening schedule.

A team of local supporters or coaches can be trained to ensure that screening measures are administered seamlessly and accurately. Written protocols that detail each step of the screening should be used to facilitate correct administration. If timed measures are used, digital count-down timers are essential to ensure accurate and consistent timing across classrooms.

EVALUATING TIER I INSTRUCTION EFFECTS AND BOLSTERING AS NEEDED

Where many students in a class do not demonstrate proficiency on the screening task, the adequacy of Tier 1 instruction must be examined further. It may be useful to

Time	Grade	Teacher Name	Class Location	Coach
7:45–8:45	Grade 1	Teacher A	Room 1-A	Coach 1
		Teacher B	Room 2-A	Coach 2
		Teacher C	Room 3-A	Coach 3
		Teacher D	Room 4-A	Coach 4
9:00–10:00	Grade 3	Teacher I	Room 1-C	Coach 1
		Teacher J	Room 2-C	Coach 2
		Teacher K	Room 3-C	Coach 3
		Teacher L	Room 4-C	Coach 4
10:15–11:15	Grade 2	Teacher E	Room 1-B	Coach 1
		Teacher F	Room 2-B	Coach 2
		Teacher G	Room 3-B	Coach 3
		Teacher H	Room 4-B	Coach 4
11:30–12:30	Grade 5	Teacher Q	Room 1-E	Coach 1
		Teacher R	Room 2-E	Coach 2
		Teacher S	Room 3-E	Coach 3 (Coach 4 organizes data for scoring)
12:30–1:15	Lunch break			
1:15–2:15	Grade 4	Teacher M	Room 1-D	Coach 1
		Teacher N	Room 2-D	Coach 2
		Teacher O	Room 3-D	Coach 3
		Teacher P	Room 4-D	Coach 4
2:15–2:45	Catch up, organize data, and dismissal			

Figure 2.2 Sample Screening Schedule.

administer additional brief class-wide assessments to identify skills prerequisite for instruction at a given grade level that have not been mastered by students. Screening data should be examined to identify patterns that might indicate a need for systemic intervention (see Table 2.2). For example, if there is a class-wide learning problem, is it confined to only one or two classrooms, or do most classrooms at a given grade level demonstrate that learning problem? Are there many grade-wide learning problems? Are certain demographic categories of students particularly at risk (e.g., students moving into the district, English-language learners, students receiving free or reduced-price lunch)? Are there shared features

DON'T FORGET
....
Screening data offer a privileged window into teaching and allow teams to work as detectives to identify potential intervention targets that will produce the greatest gains in terms of improved student learning.

for classes demonstrating class-wide learning problems (e.g., first-year teachers or veteran teachers who might be in need of updated professional development opportunities)? Screening data offer a privileged window into teaching and allow teams to work as detectives to identify potential intervention targets that will produce the greatest gains in terms of improved student learning.

When a Tier 1 learning problem has been identified, teams must identify intervention targets and prioritize those targets. Class-wide intervention can be an effective way to begin to address Tier 1 learning problems. Class-wide intervention protocols can be developed that provide for consistent periods of task demonstration (modeling), guided student practice in completing the task, and independent timed practice to build fluency over time for particular skills. These standard protocols can be used to introduce controlled instructional trials which can rapidly accelerate learning, produce generalized performance gains (i.e., as students improve skills, general instruction is enhanced or optimized), and offer teachers a model for components of instruction that may efficiently enhance learning. Implementing class-wide intervention across many grade levels is an effective way to initiate broader system change. Specifically, class-wide intervention becomes an opportunity for teams to articulate essential skills, to focus efforts on ensuring that students master these essential skills in a timely fashion, and to link student proficiency to instructional efforts in the classroom. Characteristics of effective class-wide intervention include (1) frequent monitoring of student progress, (2) using standard protocols that include elements of effective instruction, (3) monitoring the fidelity of intervention implementation, and (4) determining when to increase task difficulty based on student mastery of taught skills. Class-wide intervention provides teams a basis for troubleshooting instruction generally and for evaluating professional development and coaching efforts to resolve barriers to effective instruction in the classroom.

Where Tier 1 learning problems are identified, usually troubleshooting is required to ensure that teachers have adequate resources for instruction and that instructional interaction in the classroom is maximized in general (see Table 2.3). Where Tier 1 learning problems are detected, there are often long-standing

Table 2.2 Organizing and Examining Screening Data

Step 1	Rule out class-wide problem ⟶ (print class-wide and grade-wide graphs with criterion reference).	Proceed to individual assessment and intervention as needed
Step 2	If class-wide problem is not ruled out, consider ⟶	Was measurement task appropriate?
		Was measurement correctly administered?
		Common features of classes apparent? ⟶
			By grade?
			By content?
			By particular teachers?
			Are students being tracked?
			Demographic features of students?
	Look backward ⟶	Prerequisite skills mastered?
			Rapid increase in content difficulty or expectations for learning?

(continued)

Table 2.2 (continued)

		Look forward ⟶	Deficits apparent at subsequent grade levels?
Step 3	PRIORITIZE intervention targets.	Consider patterns and prioritize (by grade, content, demographics, others)	
Step 4	COORDINATE efforts to	Repair existing problems	
		Prevent future problems	
Step 5	EVALUATE solutions.	Monitor % of class-wide problems	
		% of grade-wide problems	
		% of students below criterion on screening (by demographic features)	

Table 2.3 Examining and Troubleshooting Instructional Basics

Troubleshoot Instructional Foundations			Solutions if "No" Is Checked
	Yes	No	
Adequate materials are available to facilitate instruction.			Ensure instructional materials are available. Ensure student assessment system is matched to instruction and is available for all students with data-tracking software.
Clearly defined essential skills in sequence.			Review standards to prioritize most important skills, specify sequence for instruction, ensure essential skills are taught to mastery.
Calendar for teaching skills.			Specify when essential skills will be taught and by which date they will be mastered for the entire year. Work with teachers to ensure teachers follow the instructional calendar to ensure all skills are taught to mastery.
Adequate instructional time is devoted to instruction, practice with feedback, and guided application.			Review time available for instruction each day in the classroom. Make adjustments based on prioritized essential skills and prioritized intervention targets.
Professional development activities provide for coaching and feedback to teacher implementation efforts.			Review professional development resources to ensure a keen focus on prioritized intervention targets.
Troubleshoot Instructional Interaction			
Task presentation clear with correct and incorrect examples of responding demonstrated for students.			Include observations in classrooms as part of personnel review.
Use of sufficient cues to provide guided practice correctly completing task (100% accuracy untimed).			Include observations in classrooms as part of personnel review.
Pacing of instruction is matched to student need.			Integrate student assessment with instructional planning. Ensure

(continued)

Table 2.3 (continued)

Troubleshoot Instructional Foundations	Yes	No	Solutions if "No" Is Checked
			software is available to organize student learning data, and provide professional development to assist teachers in translating student learning data to more effective instruction.
Degree of feedback is matched to student competence.			Integrate student assessment with instructional planning. Ensure software is available to organize student learning data, and provide professional development to assist teachers in translating student learning data to more effective instruction.
Skills are introduced according to a calendar of instruction.			Build a calendar of instruction that specifies when essential skills will be taught and by which date they will be mastered. Ensure a system for assessing student learning is in place. Assess student learning at routine intervals to ensure that skills are established by specified dates for most students. Link these skills and dates to universal screening measurement selection.
Student mastery of taught skills is assessed, and opportunities are provided for additional instruction or enrichment as needed.			Ensure there is a master calendar providing time for supplemental instruction (e.g., via Tier 2 and Tier 3). Ensure that most students master skills according to the instructional calendar.
Students are actively engaged.			Check via direct observation. If engagement is low, troubleshoot task difficulty. (Tasks may be a poor match with student capability). Actively address weak skills with class-wide intervention. Minimize transition times (less than 2 minutes per transition) and time devoted to noninstructional activities in class.

			Emphasize active student responding with feedback and incentives for high-quality work production.
Minimize time devoted to noninstructional activity (e.g., transition time).			Check via direct observation. All transitions should be less than 2 minutes. Initiate a transition routine intervention to reduce transition times due to their direct and devastating cost to instructional time and student learning outcomes.
Instructional time emphasizes practice with feedback.			Include observations in classroom as part of personnel review. Devote professional development activities to increasing active student responding.

classroom variables that have been detrimental to attaining strong learning outcomes class-wide (e.g., poor classroom management, calendar of instruction not followed, inadequate instructional time devoted to content).

PLANNING AND IMPLEMENTING TIER 2 INTERVENTIONS

Tier 2 interventions might involve standard class-wide interventions in isolated classrooms. Alternatively, standard-protocol interventions may be delivered to small groups of students who demonstrate similar baseline skill proficiencies. The term "standard protocol" refers to interventions for which the components are well specified (i.e., protocol) and have been shown to work generally for large numbers of students (i.e., standard). These are easy to build and might include interventions such as listening passage preview for reading, modeling correct problem completion, cover-copy-and compare interventions, beat-the-timer interventions, and others. Naturally occurring classroom routines offer many

DON'T FORGET

Class-wide intervention can become an opportunity for teams to:

- articulate essential skills,
- focus efforts on ensuring that students master these essential skills in a timely fashion, and
- link student proficiency to instructional efforts in the classroom.

Class-wide intervention provides teams a basis for troubleshooting instruction generally and for evaluating professional development and coaching efforts to resolve barriers to effective instruction in the classroom.

≋ Rapid Reference 2.3

Tier 2 interventions:
- Should supplement Tier 1 instruction (value added).
- Should target skills and use materials that match the students' capability level.
- Can be delivered efficiently using standard protocols or commercial products.
- Should be monitored weekly or biweekly.

opportunities for Tier 2 intervention. For example, supplemental reading supports provided via Title I services might be adjusted to permit stronger learning gains with RtI. Universal screening data might be used to identify students in need of these supports, and standard-protocol interventions

DON'T FORGET

The term "standard protocol" refers to interventions for which the components are well specified (i.e., protocol) and have been shown to work generally for large numbers of students (i.e., standard).

or a commercial supplemental reading intervention program could be provided to those students who are at risk. Additionally, where flexible grouping is occurring, universal screening data obtained at routine intervals could be used for more accurate grouping of students and more sensitive evaluation of instructional efforts for each group. Where learning gains are not sufficient, instructional troubleshooting can occur during grade-level planning meetings.

EVALUATING TIER 2 INTERVENTION EFFECTS AND BOLSTERING AS NEEDED

Where Tier 2 interventions are occurring, frequent progress monitoring is warranted. Intervention sessions should occur daily with weekly or biweekly progress monitoring data points. Two types of data should be collected to facilitate accurate decision making: direct evidence of intervention implementation and student learning data. Direct evidence of intervention implementation should be collected. Sources of this evidence could include completed worksheets, log-in records at a computer (for computer-administered intervention), a self-monitoring checklist completed by the teacher indicating that the intervention steps have been completed for the day, and a student score on an assessment activity tracking the intervention effects. Student learning data include direct assessments of the skill that is being targeted for intervention and a criterion-level skill reflecting what is expected for success in the student's classroom. For example, a student may participate in intervention to build fluency in basic subtraction facts while the criterion skill involves multidigit subtraction or word problems requiring subtraction or addition computations. It is also possible that the criterion-level skill may be the one that is targeted during intervention (e.g., when students are not far behind). To reach a decision about Tier 2 intervention effects, decision makers first need to verify that the intervention was implemented as planned and then evaluate the degree to which the intervention produced desirable changes in the student's learning under intervention conditions and under more typical classroom conditions.

PLANNING AND IMPLEMENTING TIER 3 INTERVENTIONS

Tier 3 interventions should be individualized as these represent the most intensive of intervention services that can be brought to bear on a student's learning problem within general education. Before Tier 3 intervention is implemented, data should indicate that most students are responding well to Tier 1 instruction and that Tier 2 intervention was successful for most students who were struggling and was unsuccessful for the student who will proceed to Tier 3. Moreover, student assessment data are needed before implementing a Tier 3 intervention to guide intervention development and tailor it to the student's individual learning needs. Functional academic assessment (Daly, Witt, Martens, & Dool, 1997; Daly et al., 1999; Noell et al., 1998) should be conducted to identify a student's instructional level on the series of skills within a logical hierarchy related to his or her skill deficit. Motivation effects on student learning should be ruled out via brief instructional trials with and without incentives for improved performance. The outcome of the functional academic assessment session is to identify empirically via a series of instructional trials outside of the classroom an intervention that will work if deployed properly in the classroom. Once an intervention of known effect has been identified, resources can be geared toward ensuring its adequate implementation in the child's classroom. Failing to complete a test drive of the intervention prior to implementation is a substantial and common threat to RtI decisions. Implementers should suspect that interventions are not being properly tested before deployment and implementation integrity is not being properly supported when interventions are frequently changed during the implementation period and/or high levels of intervention failures are observed.

CAUTION

Failing to complete a test drive of the intervention prior to implementation and to properly monitor and support intervention integrity are substantial and common threats to RtI decisions.

EVALUATING TIER 3 INTERVENTION EFFECTS AND BOLSTERING AS NEEDED

Tier 3 intervention sessions should occur daily with a weekly progress monitoring data point. Each week the child's performance on the targeted and criterion-level skills should be measured directly. Where performance is not improved, intervention troubleshooting should occur in this way. Intervention integrity should be assessed directly via in-class observation. This session should be used to troubleshoot intervention integrity to maximize intervention effects. If prompting and coaching are required for correct intervention implementation, then a follow-up integrity check should occur in the subsequent week to reassess and retrain for integrity as needed. If implementation integrity was adequate and student performance was accurate but slow, rewards for high-quality work production during the intervention can be added or enhanced, and the intervention can be continued another week. If intervention integrity was adequate but student errors were frequent, task difficulty may be reduced and the intervention continued for another week. As students meet criterion, difficulty of intervention materials can be advanced until the student meets criterion on the criterion-level skill.

CAUTION
....

Before Tier 3 intervention is implemented, data should indicate that most students are responding well to Tier 1 instruction and that Tier 2 intervention was successful for most students who were struggling and was unsuccessful for the student who will proceed to Tier 3. Moreover, student assessment data are needed before implementing a Tier 3 intervention to guide intervention development and tailor it to the student's individual learning needs.

LINKING RTI DATA TO RESOURCE ALLOCATION DECISIONS AND DIAGNOSTIC DECISION MAKING

Suggestions vary as to what constitutes an adequate amount of time for an intervention to have had an effect on student learning at Tier 3. Key to reaching an accurate decision here is that the intervention has been monitored frequently and managed accordingly and that sufficient data are available to forecast whether the student eventually would succeed with Tier 3 intervention. Once sufficient data are available to make this judgment, then an RtI decision should be made. It is not reasonable to conclude that an RtI decision cannot be made where the intervention has not been managed correctly and then simply do nothing (Reynolds & Shaywitz, 2009a). Such an approach represents a *misapplication* or technically inadequate application of RtI. Technically adequate RtI implementation requires that intervention integrity be managed so that decisions can occur in a timely fashion. Systems should ensure that procedures are in place to verify intervention management, to correct problems where they are detected, and, in the worst-case scenario, to take over intervention implementation in individual cases *so that delays to identification do not occur.* Time delays to decisions during RtI (i.e., who is at risk? Did the intervention resolve the problem?) generally serve as powerful signs that error has occurred in the implementation process, threatening the validity of the RtI implementation.

CAUTION

Systems should ensure that procedures are in place to verify intervention management, to correct problems where they are detected, and, in the worst-case scenario, to take over intervention implementation in individual cases *so that delays to identification do not occur.* Time delays to decisions during RtI (i.e., who is at risk? Did the intervention resolve the problem?) generally serve as powerful signs that error has occurred in the implementation process.

This chapter opened with a discussion of why technical adequacy of RtI involves a series of integrated interventions, assessments, and data interpretations or decisions at each stage. Each of these activities is necessary to conclude that RtI has occurred. Each of these activities is also an opportunity for error to occur causing the RtI implementation to be inadequate. The next chapter explains technical adequacy facets of RtI.

🐟 TEST-YOURSELF QUESTIONS 🐟

1. Are the conventional standards of reliability and validity under classical test theory pertinent to RtI adequacy? Are these conventional standards sufficient to capture the adequacy of RtI decision making?
2. What are the necessary characteristics of universal screening measures?
3. Teacher referral is an empirically supported universal screening source. True or False?
4. To ensure adequate screening information, implementers should:
   (a) Select a screening task that reflects a skill that the average student is expected to be able to do at that point in the school year.

(*continued*)

(b) Use a trained team of supporters to ensure correct screening task administration.

(c) Follow standardized screening protocols to administer the screening tasks.

(d) Use software to organize the screening data for interpretation.

(e) All of the above.

5. **When many students in a class perform below criterion on screening, a class-wide learning problem is possible and should be examined directly and addressed prior to singling out individual students for further assessment.**
   True or False?

6. **What are important characteristics of Tier 2 intervention?**

7. **Potential sources of evidence of correct intervention implementation include:**
   (a) Teacher reports that the intervention was used correctly.
   (b) Scored worksheets or completed intervention materials.
   (c) Child reports that the intervention was used correctly.
   (d) None of the above.

8. **What is the key feature of Tier 3 intervention that makes it the most intensive?**

9. **The purpose of functional academic assessment when planning Tier 3 intervention is to road test the intervention or to ensure that the intervention will work prior to investing the resources needed to deploy that intervention.**
   True or False?

10. **Time delays to decisions in the RtI process generally signify possible error in RtI implementation.**
    True or False?

Answers
1. Yes, conventional standards apply, but they are not sufficient. Classification analyses are important as are direct measures of the accuracy with which intervention procedures were carried out and decision rules were correctly applied. (See Chapter 3.)
2. Brief, reliable, accurately forecast future performance without a change to instructional programming, sensitively distinguish between students truly at risk and students truly not at risk, and tied to the local expectations for learning.
3. False. Teacher referral has been found to result in false positive and false negative identification errors. Moreover, research data suggest that a controlled intervention trial improves the equity and accuracy of the screening decision.
4. e
5. True
6. Should be a supplement to core instruction, should target skills that match the capability level of the students in the group, intervention protocols should be developed to facilitate effective delivery, and student progress should be monitored at least biweekly.
7. b
8. Tier 3 intervention is individualized, meaning that student assessment data are used to build an intervention that matches the student's individual proficiency, advances at that student's individual pace, and uses strategies that have been shown to accelerate learning for that student.
9. True
10. True

Three

HOW TO OBTAIN MEANINGFUL DATA FOR DECISION MAKING: RETHINKING TECHNICAL ADEQUACY

Evaluating and ensuring technically adequate decision making requires a shift from previous ways of thinking about measurement accuracy and validity. Response to intervention (RtI) systems of decision making have many sources of potential error, and the best way to quantify decision accuracy is by using classification analyses. Classification analyses summarize whether correct decisions were made and the cost of those decisions (and decision errors), given certain procedures (measurement materials, applied cut points, intervention facets, and outcome criteria). These analyses permit variation among sites and models in the measurement tools used and decision rules applied. Over time, classification accuracy estimates will assist practitioners in selecting the most powerful procedures for RtI decision making that come at the lowest cost (in terms of use and error).

CAUTION

Professional judgment is not a technically adequate source of data for decision making in RtI because it is highly variable among professionals, and judgments are often discordant with data. Direct indicators of intervention use, data interpretation, and student performance or response must be collected for decision making.

Why should a shift to data-based decision making occur? Some who read this book may hold fast to the value of professional judgment. The problem with professional judgment empirically is that it is highly variable among professionals, and judgments are often discordant with data. MacMillan (1998) administered a commonly used standardized battery of instruments to all 150 students who were referred to a school prereferral committee. Students were followed and their eventual classification was recorded, allowing for a direct comparison of the concordance between empirically based diagnosis according to state criteria and school-level classification according to the same criteria. MacMillan found that only 6 of the 43 students diagnosed with a mental disability using the standardized assessment battery were identified as having a mental disability by the school teams. He also found that many students were diagnosed with a learning disability when they did not meet district diagnostic criteria. These findings and others highlight a pattern in teacher referral, standardized assessment, and expert interpretation that may lead to an invalid or a faulty decision to place a child in special education. That is, once the teacher has identified a student as needing help, the goal of the decision-making team is to determine not *if* but *which* problem a student has, and classification and placement are almost certain outcomes (Ysseldyke & Thurlow, 1984). In their seminal paper on clinical decision making, Meehl and Rosen (1955) stated, "[C]linical experience and common sense must be invoked when there is nothing better to be had" (p. 213).

Many variables other than data influence decision making in schools. One of the authors of this book worked at a school district that was implementing RtI. During my first month on the job, the daughter of the district's assistant superintendent was brought to the prereferral meeting at the middle school. The assistant superintendent's wife was a much-loved and well-respected teacher at one of the elementary schools, incidentally, one where we had not begun RtI implementation. By way of further background, the father of the student being referred funded half of my salary and was somewhat skeptical of RtI. I knew the referral was coming because he had stopped by my office and indicated that he and his wife were having some struggles with his daughter since she began seventh grade; could I work with her? I met with the student and gathered some data before the prereferral meeting.

The assistant superintendent, his wife, the middle school principal, and two teacher representatives attended the meeting. They were all aligned that they wanted the student evaluated for eligibility under the category of specific learning disability (SLD). Suffice it to say that all the contingencies for me were on the side of doing the evaluation. I had every reason to evaluate this young student in terms of my own self-interests. To be viewed favorably by my new colleagues and my new boss, that would have been the right decision. To ensure continued support for my own work in the district, that would have been the right decision. To facilitate implementation of RtI at the elementary school where the student's mother was a beloved teacher, that would have been the right decision. To preserve my own time, that would have been the right decision. The contingencies were also arranged for others to support evaluation. The mother and father were very worried about their daughter and believed the evaluation would give them information that would improve the child's success at home and at school. The principal of the school had every reason to want the student to be evaluated because the child's father was his direct supervisor and a good friend to boot. This decision-making team was a compassionate team of helping professionals committed to serving students. There was only one problem with evaluating the student: The data indicated that an evaluation was not needed. Thus, an evaluation was not in the best interest of the student for these reasons: (a) It would have communicated to the student that she needed to be evaluated; (b) it could have led to an incorrect diagnosis; and (c) it would have provided no information that would have aided teachers in knowing how to best help this student learn.

> ## CAUTION
> Those who make diagnostic decisions in schools operate in a political environment, one where the decisions are, like it or not, influenced by variables that ought to have no influence.

Those who make diagnostic decisions in schools operate in a political environment, one where the decisions are, like it or not, influenced by variables that ought to have no influence. There is a legacy in eligibility determination that is hard to counteract. That legacy is:

- Undue belief in a battery of assessments that can be applied without regard to contextual variables when these contextual variables are highly unstable and relevant to correct diagnosis (e.g., instructional adequacy and child motivation)
- A desire to help along with the belief that making a SLD diagnosis will be helpful to the student
- A lack of instructional resources and tools to assist students who are struggling academically

These factors cause many school-based decision-making teams to recommend evaluation when evaluation is not warranted. There is an assumption that evaluating a child when it is not needed carries no negative consequences. *This assumption is incorrect.* Evaluations, particularly unnecessary ones, carry the cost of the evaluation itself, which can be substantial when one considers: (a) the amount of professional time required; (b) the cost of a false positive error in the diagnostic decision which can be very high and may include separating the child from his or her peer group; (c) altering the instructional program in a way that will not necessarily benefit the child; and (d) the message that a diagnosis can carry to a child about his or her capacities to learn.

≡ Rapid Reference 3.1

There is a common belief that evaluations carry little harm and should be provided to rule-out potential disability if there is the slightest concern of a student learning problem. This belief is not accurate. Unnecessary evaluations are costly to systems and children and often include procedures and measures that are not well-suited to making a rule-out decision.

Classification accuracy analyses are likely to take a prominent role within technical adequacy models of RtI, just as they have assumed a primary role in the medical literature to specify the value of certain linked diagnostic and treatment procedures (McGee, 2001). All assessment data lead to (or at least should lead to) decisions. The value of those decisions can be evaluated directly even where there is variation in the tools and decision rules that led to the decision. These analyses offer users an opportunity to quantify the accuracy of certain diagnostic procedures and then to apply those procedures in light of the potential consequences of correct and incorrect diagnosis. This emphasis on classification accuracy analyses reflects the fundamental shift from the study of methods and assessment devices to the study of methods and assessment devices as they are demonstrated to produce meaningful changes for those children they are intended to benefit. Classification analyses are a way to quantify an outcome that follows certain categorical judgments like ruling in or ruling out a diagnosis.

DON'T FORGET

All assessment data lead to (or at least should lead to) decisions. The value of those decisions can be evaluated directly even where there is variation in the tools and decision rules that led to the decision using classification accuracy analyses.

To conduct a classification analysis, continuous data must be converted to categorical data via the application of a decision rule. Children are administered the test measure and coded as either above criterion (not at risk, test-negative in our case) or below criterion (at risk, test-positive in our case). At the same time, these children are classified according to some criterion often referred to as the "gold standard" comparison. The gold standard, as the name implies, is intended to reflect a certain outcome that is not variable. (In reality, there is no gold standard in psychoeducational assessment, and this fact may be a source of error in a technical adequacy model.) For example, the criterion for comparison or gold standard might be SLD diagnosis (with children sorted as meeting or not meeting diagnostic criteria for SLD). Then if you imagine a grid (see Figure 3.1), you can

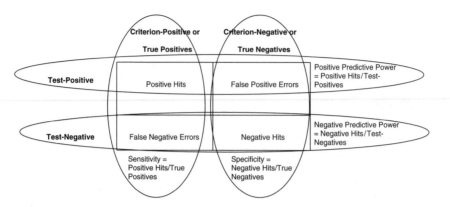

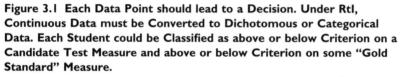

Figure 3.1 Each Data Point should lead to a Decision. Under RtI, Continuous Data must be Converted to Dichotomous or Categorical Data. Each Student could be Classified as above or below Criterion on a Candidate Test Measure and above or below Criterion on some "Gold Standard" Measure.

see that children can be sorted into four cells: test-positive and criterion-positive (decision agreements), test-positive and criterion-negative (decision disagreements), test-negative and criterion-positive (decision disagreements), test-negative and criterion-negative (decision agreements). The number of decision agreements can be divided by the total number of cases in all cells to give users an overall index of decision agreement between the two methods. These types of data can be used to evaluate the predictive value of certain symptoms or behaviors to indicate outcomes that are relevant to diagnostic decision making in education (e.g., some risk symptoms indicating long-term reading failure or a behavior indicating drop out). Classification analyses are grounded in the logic of conditional probabilities.

CONDITIONAL PROBABILITIES

Conditional probabilities provide an indication of the degree to which one observed behavior or event tends to occur in temporal proximity to the occurrence of another observed behavior or event. Conditional probabilities answer the question: When certain conditions or behaviors are observed, what is the probability that a particular behavior will either precede or follow the occurrence of these conditions (i.e., probability)? The mathematical depiction of this relationship is called a conditional probability (Bakeman & Gottman, 1986). In essence, conditional probability data are correlational data that offer the assessment team an opportunity to identify particular conditions that are most associated with particular behaviors. This technology has been most widely applied through descriptive analysis methods in behavior analysis where students are observed in the classroom and specific antecedent and consequent variables and child responses are recorded within a time-based recording system. These data allow the assessment team to identify antecedent and consequent variables that most frequently occur in close temporal proximity to certain child responses (e.g., the occurrence of aggression may be highly correlated with escape from task demands). Based on these data, the assessment team may hypothesize that a causal relationship exists between escape and aggression such that the student exhibits aggression to escape demands in the classroom. Similarly, conditional probabilities can be used to quantify the probability of the occurrence of adaptive behaviors or outcomes under RtI models. For example, conditional probabilities might reflect the degree to which positive learning trends reliably follow certain instructional conditions or levels of intervention implementation integrity. Conditional probabilities might be used to quantify the effect of intervention on diagnosis of SLD or the potential of certain learning deficits (or intervention response characteristics) to signify the presence of SLD.

CAUTION

To ensure diagnostic accuracy, specific and unique markers must be identified that lead reliably to diagnosis. A failure to consider the degree to which certain characteristics are *uniquely* associated with a particular diagnosis is a common problem in psychological diagnosis in general.

Conditional probabilities are highly influenced by the base rate occurrence of specific behaviors or events, and so-called spurious correlations are probable. To ensure diagnostic accuracy, specific and unique markers must be identified that lead reliably to diagnosis. For example, poor reading performance may be associated with teacher referral for a special education evaluation. With access to universal screening data, one may detect that nearly all students in the potential referral population demonstrate poor reading performance. Hence, the conditional probability of referral following poor reading performance may be quite high but at the same time may be useless as a marker of the need for referral for evaluation. For poor reading performance to be useful for making a referral decision, it must be associated with referral and not associated with nonreferral (Campbell & Fiske, 1959). This scenario is not possible where large numbers of children demonstrate low reading performance (VanDerHeyden, Witt, & Barnett, 2005). A failure to consider the degree to which certain characteristics are *uniquely* associated with a particular diagnosis is a common problem in psychological diagnosis in general and has resulted in very poor classification agreements (Gresham & Gansle, 1992) and widespread criticism on categorical service delivery in special education (Reynolds, 1991). An overreliance on nonspecific measures for SLD created many of the technical problems reported with its diagnosis (Lennon & Slesinski, 1999; Stuebing et al., 2002; Vellutino et al., 1996; Vellutino, Scanlon, & Tanzman, 1998). For example, the degree to which poor reading performance may be associated with conditions other than SLD (e. g., lack of instruction, lack of motivation) reduces its value as a unique, specific, and accurate marker for SLD (Stuebing et al., 2002).

One lesson to be learned from the conditional probabilities literature in behavioral assessment is that the reliability estimates for measured symptoms or behaviors may be highly variable and systematically overestimated where base rate occurrences are high and systematically underestimated where base rate occurrences are low (Kazdin, 1982). Researchers and practitioners who wish to use conditional probability-based calculations (such as those described in this book) to determine predictive values of certain assessments or interventions must consider basic methodological issues, including clear operational definitions with demonstrated reliability. For example, the salience of a symptom or the ease with which a symptom can be measured may unduly inflate its measured occurrence relative to less well-defined variables and inflate the conditional probability estimates.

CLASSIFICATION AGREEMENTS

In their seminal article, Meehl and Rosen (1955) described how conditional probabilities of certain symptoms and prevalence of disorders may affect diagnostic accuracy. Meehl and Rosen applied Bayes' theorem to diagnostic accuracy and illustrated how base rate or prevalence of a condition (e.g., SLD) affects the probability of an accurate prediction using certain symptoms of known predictive value. Many readers are familiar with the classic example of marbles in urns to illustrate Bayes' theorem. Suppose there are two urns, one of which contains 80% black marbles and one that contains 30% black marbles. Now suppose that the probability of drawing a marble from the first urn is 20% and the probability of drawing a marble from the second urn is 80%. If a blindfolded person selects a marble that turns out to be black, what is the probability that the marble came from the first urn? Many people mistakenly predict that the marble came from the first urn because of the very high "symptom" rate (high number of black marbles) when the actual probability of the marble coming from the first urn is computed as 40%, which means that the prediction just given would be correct less than half the time, or worse than chance.

Meehl and Rosen argue that base rates that diverge from 50% (equal chance of drawing from each urn or equal prevalence of those who have and those who do not have a diagnosed condition that that test is trying to predict), the base rate will exert undue influence on the predictive value of a screening measure or symptom. Returning to the previous example, in a classroom where 90% of the students actually have reading difficulties due to poor instruction, even a very precise and accurate measurement tool designed to detect reading difficulties will be unimpressive in context (i.e., likely to be less useful than just assuming all students have reading difficulties, which would be a 10% error rate). Many diagnosticians in research and practice underestimate the effect of base rates. Classification agreement analyses can be used to quantify decision accuracy in terms of its impact on outcomes in situations with particular base rates. The most commonly used classification agreement estimates include sensitivity, specificity, positive predictive power, and negative predictive power.

Sensitivity and Specificity

Sensitivity and specificity characterize a measure and in theory are stable regardless of the conditions under which the measure is applied. Because each assessment finding should lead to a decision, to compute classification agreement analyses and evaluate the value of the decisions made, users need a criterion assessment with an agreed-on cut score (i.e., gold standard) to indicate the "true" positive (student diagnosed when should be diagnosed) and "true" negative (student not diagnosed when should not be diagnosed) cases in the measurement sample. Users also need a test measure for which a cut point can be applied to yield test-positive and test-negative findings to be compared to the criterion measure. It is useful to think of a grid of four cells (see Figure 3.1) where every case can be considered criterion-positive (true positive) or criterion-negative (true negative) and test-positive or test-negative. Sensitivity is the power of a test to identify true positives and is computed as the number of test and criterion positives (cases that are positive on both the criterion and test measures) divided by the total number of criterion positives (or true positives). Specificity is the power of a test to identify true negatives and is computed as the number of test and criterion negatives (cases that are negative on both the criterion and test measures) divided by the total number of criterion negatives (true negatives).

CAUTION

In a classroom where 90% of the students actually have reading difficulties due to poor instruction, even a very precise and accurate measurement tool designed to detect reading difficulties will be unimpressive in that context (i.e., likely to be less useful than just assuming all students have reading difficulties, which would be a 10% error rate). Many diagnosticians in research and practice underestimate the effect of base rates.

Obviously, the value of the sensitivity and specificity estimates depend on a number of variables including correct selection and administration of a criterion measure. In these estimates in the medical literature, sensitivity and specificity are static variables based on outcomes that are fairly unarguable, such as mortality or blood culture values. In education, the so-called outcome variables often lie on a continuum where researchers or practitioners must set a cut score for interpretation. The placement of the cut scores may be debatable (and is at least a fixed element pertinent to future replications and interpretations). In other words, comparison of sensitivity and specificity values are tied to the criterion selected and the cut score applied; comparing sensitivity and specificity values across studies is difficult unless the criterion and cut score are the same. The use of a given measure to reflect a particular outcome may also be debatable, and measurement features may influence the data points (e.g., positively skewed performance distributions on the test or criterion measure may systematically influence sensitivity and specificity estimates).

Importantly, for diagnostic decision making, the presence of some indicators will have more value for certain types of decisions, but others have more value when absent, depending on the associated measure's sensitivity and specificity. Indicators with high specificity (e.g., measure identifies high proportion of true negatives—students whose data indicate sufficient learning and who do not have a serious learning problem) when present are useful for ruling in a disorder (e.g., SLD). Indicators with high sensitivity (e.g., measure identifies high proportion of true positives or students whose data indicate insufficient learning and who do have a serious learning problem) when absent are useful for ruling out a disorder (e.g., SLD). The use of sensitivity and specificity estimates must be quantified for different diagnostic data sets and decisions so that practitioners can make a relative judgment about which types of data collected under which types of conditions are useful for particular diagnostic decisions.

Two types of data are readily available with most RtI models:

1. Universal screening data should be available for all children in the school to determine risk.
2. Response to intervention data should be available for children who are found to be at risk during the initial screening.

We can calculate estimates of specificity and sensitivity from an existing data set (VanDerHeyden, Witt, & Naquin, 2003) to illustrate the point. Using the screening criterion (below the 16th percentile in a class and in the frustration range; Deno & Mirkin, 1977), a subset of children are identified as at risk. Following this procedure, children could be coded as screen-positive (indicating a difficulty) or screen-negative (no difficulty noted). All screen-positive children participate in additional assessment to examine the effects of incentives on performance followed by a single instructional trial as a proxy of RtI. Following this procedure, children could be coded as RtI-positive or RtI-negative. Concurrently, all children are provided with a package of criterion measures including the Iowa Test of Basic Skills and curriculum-based assessment with 5 to 7 intervention standard protocol intervention sessions. Hence, sensitivity of the screening criterion just described was .94. Specificity was .54.

≡ Rapid Reference 3.2

Measures with high sensitivity when negative (i.e., measured symptom is absent) are useful for ruling *out* a disorder or condition.

Measures with high specificity when positive (i.e., measured symptom is present) are useful for ruling *in* a disorder.

The follow-up assessment that included an assessment of the effect of incentives on performance and a single instructional session decreased sensitivity but increased specificity. Specificity of screening plus incentives plus a single instructional session was .89. Sensitivity of screening plus incentives plus a single instructional session was .76. Hence, use of the screening criterion alone was supported to make a rule-out decision when a child was screen-negative (i.e., performs above the screening criterion). These data also indicate that the use of the screening criterion alone was *not* useful for ruling in the presence of a disorder like SLD. Symptoms that can be measured with greater specificity when present are useful to rule in a diagnosis. Hence, the screen plus incentives plus instructional session has more utility for ruling in a disorder than does the screening criterion alone. This finding is consistent with Meehl and Rosen's (1955) suggestion to use a "successive hurdles" approach to decision making where individuals are subjected to further assessment based on earlier more sensitive assessments. The successive hurdles approach is widely used in screening (where false negative errors are avoided at a cost to false positive errors) and is consistent with RtI decision making (Jenkins, Hudson, & Johnson, 2007).

Importantly, each time a new decision is faced, the prevalence rates change. Thus, those who wish to make valid decisions must again adjust their priorities for sensitive versus specific measures and reevaluate the utility of various symptoms in the context of new prevalence or base rates. For example, when a screening has ruled out 85% of students, the remaining pool of 15% of students is likely to contain high base rates of many of the symptom indicators and certainly a higher prevalence of "true" SLD than did the original sample.

≡ Rapid Reference 3.3

In gated decision models like RtI, each time a decision rule is applied to filter the sample, the prevalence or base rates for the remaining subset of students changes. Users must readjust their measurement selection, decision rules, and predictive accuracy estimates (especially positive and negative predictive power) accordingly.

Positive and Negative Predictive Power

Whereas sensitivity and specificity estimates indicate which tests or data sets will be most useful, positive and negative predictive power provide users with an idea of the probability of an accurate decision. Knowing that a test detects 95% of true positives in a population (sensitivity) does not allow the diagnostician to tell the individual who has just tested positive what the chances are that the diagnosis is correct. Positive and negative predictive values often are referred to as diagnostic efficiency estimates because they provide an indication of a score's or symptom's utility in making a diagnostic decision. Positive predictive power (sometimes referred to as positive predictive value) is the probability that a positive test result is truly positive. Negative predictive power (sometimes referred to as negative predictive value) is the probability that a negative test result is truly negative.

However, predictive power estimates are highly dependent on the base rates or prevalence rates of a given disorder. Therefore, high positive predictive power estimates may indicate strong positive predictive power (utility of a symptom for ruling in a disorder), high prevalence of a disorder, or both. Similarly, high negative predictive power may indicate strong negative predictive power (utility of a symptom for ruling out a disorder), low prevalence of a disorder, or both (Weissler, 1999).

Rapid Reference 3.4

Negative predictive power and positive predictive power are highly dependent on or influenced by prevalence or base rates.

Understanding these nuances of predictive power is necessary to developing meaningful risk models where the prevalence of the "criterion" condition may vary substantially (e.g., SLD diagnosis versus high risk for reading failure). Typically, disorder prevalence is estimated based on some direct incidence data on an index population. In the case of RtI analyses, prevalence of SLD is a key variable in conducting meaningful outcome analyses. If the prevalence value is set at 10%, then different conclusions about the utility of various symptoms in making a diagnosis might be made than if the prevalence value were set at 3%. Based on existing research data, a prevalence value of SLD might be 3% to 5% of the school-age population. Drastically different positive and negative predictive power estimates can arise based on rather subtle differences between samples. Hence, it is unwise to compare these values across studies and reach conclusions about certain symptoms having greater utility than others.

Rapid Reference 3.5

In reaching a diagnosis, negative predictive power and positive predictive power estimates should not be compared across studies to reach conclusions about relative symptom value.

DERIVATION OF DECISION RULES OR CUT POINTS

Because the test usually yields data that are continuous and then a decision rule is applied to these data to characterize the test as positive or negative, the decision rule may be specified and then adjusted to maximize correct positive findings or correct negative findings. To gain correct positive findings generally requires the loss of correct negative findings (and vice versa), and so the predictive power estimates are highly interrelated. Figures 3.2 and 3.3 illustrate this principle. A scatter plot can be generated showing each student's score on the test (y-axis) and criterion (x-axis) measure. The cut point on the x-axis measure is static and reflects the desired outcome, in this example, meeting the proficiency criterion on the year-end accountability measure. The "test" measure scores appear on the y-axis, in this case oral reading fluency scores obtained during universal screening in the spring. A vertical line is drawn through the cut score indicating proficiency on the criterion measure (x-axis). This line is static and does not move. A horizontal line may be drawn from the y-axis creating four quadrants on the graph. The horizontal line can be moved up and down the y-axis to identify the score on the "test measure" that creates the best prediction (with desired errors occurring relative to the purpose of the decision being made). Receiver operating curve (ROC)* analyses may be used on datasets of this type to identify the point of equilibrium where false negative and false positive errors are minimized.

As noted previously, the value of any cut point is influenced by the degree to which the criterion measure represented the "right" outcome and accurately measured that outcome and the degree to which the test represented the right content of appropriate difficulty. Correlation between scores may be strong while decision accuracy is inadequate (Good, Simmons, & Kame'enui, 2001; Jenkins et al., 2007). Normal score distributions are desirable for the predictor and criterion variables. For example, a negatively skewed distribution and high mean score may unfairly maximize sensitivity.

In setting cut points for categorization, users must consider the purpose of the decision that will be made, particularly with respect to changing prevalence or base rates occurring as samples are filtered down in a series of sequential assessments (i.e., from screening to those receiving Tier 2 intervention to those receiving Tier 3 intervention). A common mistake seems to be deriving a cut point on a sample and then reporting the classification agreements and analysis data to support the utility of the procedure being tested. This approach overestimates predictive accuracy (Campbell & Fiske, 1959) and should be avoided. Cross-validation must be conducted to identify cut points of enduring and large-scale utility. Even so, what is likely to result are cut points that are appropriate for certain decisions in certain contexts rather than very general cut points that can be applied in most contexts.

---

*For further ROC information, see the Authors' Note beginning on page 146.

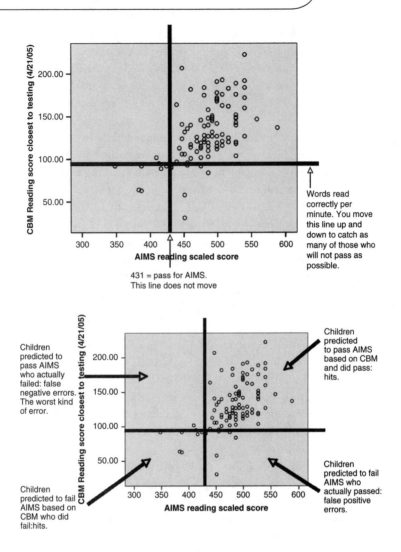

Figures 3.2 and 3.3 Illustrate the Identification of a Decision Rule for Determining Risk Status on a Test Measure. Each Child's Performance can be Plotted Using a Scatter Plot where the Student's Test Score (CBM) is on the y-axis and the Student's Score on the Criterion Measure (e.g., year-end Accountability Measure) is on the x-axis. The Decision Rule for the Criterion Measure is Typically Static. The Decision Rule can be Adjusted (on the y-axis) to Maximize Correct Decisions and Minimize Incorrect Decisions Relative to the Decision that is being Made.

SOURCES OF ERROR IN RTI: CHARACTERISTICS OF THE UNDERLYING DATA SET THAT AFFECT DECISION-MAKING ANALYSES

One troubling aspect of RtI is that it provides many opportunities for error that could lead to faulty decisions. RtI requires efficient and effective universal screening, identification, and progress monitoring procedures to (a) identify students who need additional services, (b) provide data to guide intervention selection, and (c) provide data regarding the effectiveness (or lack thereof) of the intervention. Each of these decisions (and the associated assessment and intervention procedures) creates opportunities for errors that ultimately compromise the technical adequacy of an RtI model. The errors may be procedural (related to poor integrity of implementation or incorrect administration of measures), measurement centered (scores obtained are not reliable or meaningfully correlated with valued outcomes), or related to data interpretation (data are misinterpreted, decision rules are not correctly applied). These errors could occur in isolation or in clusters to have a cumulative effect on technical adequacy. Finally, each decision at each stage is then used iteratively to inform the procedures, measures, and interpretations that follow; hence, the timing of an error may relate systematically to how detrimental the error is to the adequacy of an RtI model.

Table 3.1 lists the series of steps that are required for RtI implementation, including:

1. Screen all students.
2. Determine risk.
3. Identify patterns.
4. Link screening data to resource allocation decisions for prevention.
5. Determine Tier 2 or 3 interventions.
6. Select and implement interventions.
7. Evaluate intervention effects.
8. Troubleshoot intervention effects.
9. Judge intervention outcome.
10. Link to resource allocation decisions for remediation.

Each action has associated opportunities for error. In the column next to the action are listed potential sources of error that could cause RtI users to reach inaccurate decisions. Errors associated with each action primarily involve inaccurate measurement, inaccurate intervention implementation, and incorrect data interpretation. Each of these is discussed in detail in the next section.

Table 3.1 Sources of Error in RtI

RtI Component	Source of Error	Signs that Error May Have Occurred
Screen all students	Measure not reliable, valid, sensitive	Nonvalidated tool selected for use.
		Scores inconsistent over short intervals of time where instruction would not be expected to have caused much change.
	Measure incorrectly administered.	Digital timers not used.
		Scored screening protocols unavailable.
	Data incorrectly interpreted.	Any number of children for whom no decision has been made after 30 days.
		Children below criterion at screening who did not receive intervention.
		Children with failed RtI who are not referred for further assessment.
		Children with successful RtI who are referred for further assessment.
Determine risk	Cut point not efficient.	High numbers of false positive errors.
		Consider "successive hurdles" to improve efficiency.
	Cut point not accurate.	Use of normative data only.
		Benchmark criteria should also be applied.
	Cut point incorrectly applied.	Children above criterion receiving intervention.
		Children below criterion not receiving intervention.

RtI Component	Source of Error	Signs that Error May Have Occurred
		Too few students receive intervention (fewer than 10% of students receiving Tier 2 or 3 intervention).
		Delay to intervention implementation (more than 30 days from initial risk decision to intervention implementation).
Identify patterns	Data not examined to identify class-wide, grade-wide, and school-wide learning problems.	School-wide, grade-wide, and class-wide performance problems apparent on consecutive screenings.
	Data not examined to identify performance differences by demographics.	Disaggregated findings unavailable.
	Frequency of assessment has not been increased to track pattern resolution.	Screening fewer than 3 times per year.
Link to resource allocation decisions	Evaluation did not occur for core instructional programs, calendar of instruction, and professional development where school-wide and grade-wide problems were apparent.	Greater than 20% of students performed below criterion on consecutive screenings.
	Screening data were not used to distribute supplemental instructional resources.	Children in risk range on consecutive screenings.
	Screening data were not used to evaluate supplemental instructional resources.	Children who received supplemental instruction remain in risk range on consecutive screenings.
Determine Tier 2 or 3 interventions	Tier 2 interventions were not implemented where indicated (class-wide learning problems, small groups) prior to beginning Tier 3 intervention.	Tier 3 interventions implemented for greater than 10% of screened population.
Select and implement intervention	Intervention integrity including accuracy, consistency, and duration of implementation.	Delay to intervention outcome decision (greater than 30 days from intervention implementation to intervention outcome decision).

(continued)

Table 3.1 (continued)

RtI Component	Source of Error	Signs that Error May Have Occurred
		No intervention protocols available, no integrity data available.
		Tier 2 interventions unsuccessful for greater than 20% of those exposed to such interventions (10% of screened population).
		Tier 3 interventions unsuccessful for greater than 10% of those exposed to such interventions (5% of screened population).
Evaluate intervention effects	Progress monitoring data not reliable, valid, and sensitive.	Tier 2 interventions unsuccessful for greater than 20% of those exposed to such interventions (10% of screened population).
		Tier 3 interventions unsuccessful for greater than 10% of those exposed to such interventions (5% of screened population).
	Progress monitoring data incorrectly administered (at each occasion).	Highly variable data points from week to week.
	Progress monitoring data insufficient to inform decision (not enough data, not collected at routine intervals).	More than a week between progress monitoring data points.

Fewer than 3 progress monitoring data points. |
| Troubleshoot intervention effects | Intervention integrity has not been measured. | No integrity data available. |
| | Intervention integrity not sufficient. | Integrity data suggest implementation did not occur |

RtI Component	Source of Error	Signs that Error May Have Occurred
		correctly and interventionist was not retrained with performance feedback follow-up documented.
	Intervention incorrectly selected (materials too challenging or too easy, individualized rewards not provided, corrective feedback not matched to student need).	Highly variable child performance during intervention may signal integrity or motivation problem that requires troubleshooting. Poor growth may signal need to adjust intervention by reducing task difficulty and increasing antecedent support for correct responding and frequency/immediacy of corrective feedback. Strong growth but below criterion performance may indicate need to advance difficulty level of materials, support fluent skill development further through use of incentives, and maximizing opportunities to respond. Poor generalization may signal the need for antecedent supports and opportunities to practice generalizing the training skill, increasing task variation, and fading of supports to more natural conditions.
Judge intervention outcome	Judgment does not account for poor integrity.	Many failed responses to intervention (incidence greater than 5% of screened population).
	Intervention incomplete before judgment is made	Fewer than 10 consecutive intervention sessions implemented with integrity following troubleshooting.
	No troubleshooting of the intervention occurred.	Highly variable data patterns.

(continued)

Table 3.1 (continued)

RtI Component	Source of Error	Signs that Error May Have Occurred
	Judgment incorrect (i.e., does not correspond to data collected).	Children with successful RtI referred for evaluation. Children with unsuccessful RtI not referred for evaluation. Children without a decision in 30 days.
Link to resource allocation decisions	Referral for additional assessment and evaluation suggested when failed RtI occurs.	Children with unsuccessful RtI not referred for evaluation.
	No referral for additional assessment and evaluation suggested when successful RtI occurs.	Children with successful RtI referred for evaluation.
	Brief meeting with teacher and parent to communicate RtI outcome, collaborate on, and share resource plan for student	Graph showing student performance relative to classmates and some criterion, graph showing performance during intervention, and intervention protocol included in child's permanent folder.

RELIABLE AND CONTEXTUALIZED DEPENDENT VARIABLE MEASUREMENT

Conventions of reliable measurement with which most psychologists and diagnosticians are fluent will continue to be relevant to assessment within RtI (American Educational Research Association, American Psychological Association, & the National Council for Measurement in Education, 1999). However, given the emphasis on trend analysis, new standards for repeated measurement and standards for adequately determining slope will need to be established. Two approaches to generating reliable measurement have relevance here, and there is no clear winner between the two. Ideally, research in this area will create a hybrid of the two logic models to measure child responding.

One logic model typified by single-subject methods allows for the collection of individually meaningful data that are of interest to teachers and parents. The second logic model, typified by nomothetic methods, allows for the identification of generalizable principles, procedures, and decision rules. Hybrid methods that allow for individual problem solving but place the response in the context of broader normative samples are necessary to build widely applicable decision-making models that have a high probability of improving outcomes of individual students. The crux of the difference between the two logic models is how each views measured performance. Single-subject methods consider a behavior or symptom, such as number of words read correctly per minute, as a *behavior*, whereas nomothetic methods view words read correctly per minute as a *score*. Within RtI, measured symptoms, such as number of words read correctly per minute, is both a behavior and a score. If number of words read correctly per minute is a behavior, then we seek to understand the conditions that control its occurrence. As a behavior, each instance or occurrence has meaning. There are no outlier performances, for example. There are only performances for which we have not identified the instructional conditions that control their occurrence; stated another way, there are only performances that we do not understand why they occurred. As a behavior, variation is desirable, and meaning comes from the ability to adequately sample the stimulus or independent variable conditions that might affect the behavior (e.g., incentives, repeated exposure to the task, task difficulty) and then to reliably produce or replicate the behavior change. As a score, however, variation is less desirable. Where we wish to reach generalized conclusions about a passage's difficulty, for example, or an intervention's general effect on learning, it is desirable to minimize variability caused by sources (e.g., reading passage characteristics) other than those of interest in the study (e.g., student capability). Outlier data points may be ignored or transformed because they do not contribute to an understanding of a general response to an independent variable manipulation.

An item with a certain feature that is inconsistently answered correctly in large test samples might be viewed as a bad item under a nomothetic model, whereas at the individual level, if the error is consistently reproducible for an individual, it might provide specific information to guide a minor instructional modification to improve learning for that individual student. In a sense, perfect measurement under a nomothetic logic model may be *perfectly insensitive* measurement under a single-subject model. Alternatively, perfect measurement under a single-subject logic model may be perfectly ungeneralizable. Certainly the conflict that lies at the heart of these two sources of evidence has been widely discussed at length in literature pertaining to how best to identify evidence-based practices or the value of various types of data for reaching decisions about the value of specific interventions (Feuer, Towne, & Shavelson, 2002; Odom et al., 2005; Schulte, 2008).

The need for both sensitive and generalizable understanding of child learning requires a blended approach. The sensitivity of the measures will need to vary to suit the desired purpose. For example, single-subject methods should be utilized to examine the effect of incentives on performance. If you want to know whether to offer incentives to a particular child in a particular classroom, it makes no sense to assess the performance of a large sample, provide incentives to all children, and then reach conclusions about the general effect of incentives on child performance based on changes in average performance—at least not if the goal is to determine whether incentives ought to be part of an intervention plan for an individual student. The decision that follows the assessment data with respect to use or nonuse of incentives can be evaluated through classification agreement analyses where the value of that decision can be quantified in terms of the degree to which it was associated with improved intervention effects. Given similar average performances with and without incentives, such data may illustrate that not all children's performances are sensitive to performance contingencies and that practice effects are minimal; but these data do not permit the conclusion that incentives have no utility.

Importantly, quantification of performance can no longer occur in isolation. Understanding of child performance is contextualized in RtI decision models. So instead of asking "What is the child's performance?" the relevant question becomes "What is the child's performance in response to particular conditions?" The range of conditions that affect student responding can be broad, and it is largely unknown how particular variations might affect the decisions and therefore the outcomes attained with RtI. Contextualized assessment of child performance does not attribute variation to error but rather seeks to understand the sources that caused the variation in the first place. A number of contextual variables can be expected to affect the technical adequacy of response measurement under RtI. Task characteristics are described in the next section to illustrate how task difficulty (an independent variable facet) may influence data obtained, decisions reached, and outcome of an RtI implementation.

Task Characteristics

Scores must be examined relative to certain task parameters including task difficulty, task sampling, and characteristics of the measure or materials used. The difficulty of the task should be determined based on (a) the purpose of the assessment, (b) what has been instructed in class or what learning expectations are in place in the instructional environment both currently and within a continuum representing year-end objectives, and (c) student ability. Tasks that are too easy or too difficult will not be sensitive to detect differences between students (affecting screening decisions) and effects of certain instructional or motivational manipulations (affecting intervention selection decisions). Moreover, tasks that are too easy will certainly lead to over- or underestimated predictive power estimates (Jenkins et al., 2007; Meehl & Rosen, 1955). Consideration should be given to the range of stimuli represented on a measure as it interacts with the purpose of the assessment. Because curriculum-based measurement provides data that are highly specific to performance of certain skills, it will be important to ensure that the relevant stimuli or problem types are included on a given measure (Fuchs & Deno, 1991). If the purpose is to monitor growth throughout the academic year toward important year-end objectives, then the measure must sample skills that will be taught throughout the year to model growth adequately. Further, the degree to which characteristics of the measure (e.g., arrangement of stimuli (Christ & Vining, 2006), the probe duration or timing (Fuchs et al, 1993)), and the thresholds or boundaries that govern the degree to which performance on such measures are predictive of identified outcomes that have functional meaning for children are largely unknown.

INTERVENTION

The independent variable in RtI is the instruction that occurs at each stage of decision making. Correct implementation or management of interventions (timing, sequencing, match to the problem, and iterative troubleshooting to enhance effectiveness) is the linchpin of RtI. This feature is part of what distinguishes RtI from traditional static assessments of learning. Traditionally, intervention variables have been ignored in psychological assessment (Gresham, 1991; Gresham et al., 1993; Noell & Gansle, 2006). Because RtI has the potential to provide contextualized data about student learning and potential for learning, the instructional conditions must be quantified *and* manipulated to yield the data on which an RtI decision can be based. That is, if practitioners are to measure what child performances are possible rather than what child performances simply are present at the time of assessment, then the independent variable becomes a critical feature of a technically adequate RtI model (VanDerHeyden, 2005). The only way to know what performance is possible given optimal learning conditions with a child is to deliver without question optimal learning conditions and measure the child's response. By analogy, we may know that a given antibiotic produces a decrease in illness symptoms for a majority of cases with similar symptoms, but to know for sure if the antibiotic will cure a particular person's illness, we must administer the antibiotic and monitor illness symptoms and respond accordingly. In fact, this type of iterative troubleshooting has led some researchers to state that it is the interventionist or teacher who must be responsive within RtI models (Olson et al., 2007).

DON'T FORGET

Because RtI has the potential to provide contextualized data about student learning and potential for learning, the instructional conditions must be quantified *and* manipulated to yield the data on which an RtI decision can be based. That is, if practitioners are to measure what child performances are possible rather than what child performances simply are present at the time of assessment, then the independent variable becomes a critical feature of a technically adequate RtI model.

To generate useful guidelines about intervention, empirical quantification of the instruction's effect on outcomes is needed. These data would provide a basis for understanding the intervention facets that matter and would become the minimal required independent variable standards in a technical adequacy model of RtI. Intervention facets that might matter include strength, duration, frequency, content, task materials, and level of individualization. Conditional probabilities and classification agreement analyses make evaluation of particular sequences of events (instructional manipulations—child response—instructional feedback) possible. Because RtI assessments require contextualized and iterative decisions, independent variable facets must be examined in tandem with dependent variable facets that might matter. Well-controlled research studies provide evidence about which instructional arrangements might work (Odom et al., 2005), and individual implementations can ensure that the intervention is matched well to the student's needs (Barnett, Daly, Jones, & Lentz, 2004; Jones & Wickstrom, 2002). Classification agreement analyses can be used to generate estimates of the degree to which certain interventions implemented under certain conditions produce favorable outcomes (or not) and at what cost. These analyses eventually might permit educators to estimate in advance given certain measured characteristics of a child and a child's learning environment which intervention strategy (delivered at what intensity) will give the highest probability of the best outcome.

CAUTION

···

A major source of potential and likely error is the misinterpretation or misuse of collected data. Even if the data have been collected correctly, multiple decision points represent opportunities for errors that will compromise the adequacy of the final RtI decision.

ACCURACY OR FIDELITY OF DATA-BASED DECISION MAKING

A major source of potential and likely error is the misinterpretation or misuse of collected data. Even if the data have been correctly collected, multiple decision points represent opportunities for errors that will compromise the adequacy of the final RtI decision. MacMillan and colleagues (1998/1999) found that school-based assessment teams rarely reached decisions that (a) matched with their own data, (b) matched with independently collected data, or (c) met local and state standards for diagnostic decisions. VanDerHeyden, Witt, and Gilbertson (2007) implemented an RtI model in a district as a prereferral process with systematic procedures for presenting the RtI data to the referral decision-making team. Team decisions were monitored, permitting an analysis of the degree to which the teams reached decisions that were supported by the RtI data collected at each site. Essentially, these authors found that in the first year of implementation, decision makers tended to refer for evaluation all children who demonstrated an inadequate RtI (representing data-consistent decisions) but also decided to refer for evaluation approximately half of the cases that were exposed to Tier 3 intervention but had a successful RtI (representing data-inconsistent decisions). These findings illustrate that variables other than the RtI data influenced the team's decision to refer for evaluation. So as long as unoperationalized variables influence human decision making, "errors" in data interpretation will be highly probable. This reality represents a significant threat to technically adequate RtI implementation.

Returning to Table 3.1, the last column provides signs that error may have occurred. Readers who wish to evaluate potential threats to valid decision making in their RtI implementations might consider whether any of these signs are present in their implementation. Careful checking to ensure that no signs of error are present enhances the believability of the data and the reliability of the judgments made. In the remainder of this chapter, we make recommendations for the selection of screening materials and decision rules, evaluation of intervention implementation, progress monitoring, and evaluating intervention outcomes.

RECOMMENDATIONS FOR TECHNICALLY ADEQUATE SCREENING

Materials

Research supports the use of screening materials that reflect skills that students are expected to have mastered at that point in the program of instruction. Content-controlled materials that are external to the curriculum are preferred for several reasons. Materials that are designed for assessment purposes contain stimuli that are controlled only to reflect the difficulty level being assessed, and the content is arranged in an order that does not present a threat to the results (e.g., more difficult items first, more difficult items and fewer easy items, and vice versa). It is also important that students not have access to the screening materials outside of the screening session. Otherwise the scores obtained during screening may be inflated by practice effects. A variety of commercial products are available for screening. The key factor is to ensure that the measure has evidence of reliability, has the sensitivity to detect students at risk at the lowest cost to efficiency (i.e., false positive identification errors), and reflects skills that are expected according to the local standards for performance at that time of year. Curriculum-based measurements (CBM) were suggested in Chapter 2.

Role of Slope and Level Estimates

Because slope presents technical challenges that threaten conclusions from the data, we suggest that level estimates alone serve as the basis for the screening decision. Use of a level-alone criterion for screening is empirically supported (Jenkins et al., 2007; Schatschneider, Wagner, & Crawford, 2008; Speece, 2005). Further, a single trial or single score from CBM is supported as an adequate basis for reaching a screening decision (Ardoin et al., 2004; VanDerHeyden et al., 2003). The use of a single-trial CBM score can be used to reach a rule-out decision such as is desired at screening. New RtI criteria can and should be adopted as the research progresses. Promising research is under way at the time this book was written to develop methods and recommendations for accurate measurement of slope (Ardoin & Christ, 2008).

Empirically Supported Decision Rules for Screening

A decision rule that uses both a benchmark criterion and a normative criterion should be used. The value of a benchmark criterion is that it has functional meaning for all those who score below that criterion. The criterion might predict who will and will not pass the year-end accountability measure, which is inextricably tied to consequential validity. (Findings will have immediate and consequential implications for students in the classroom.) For example, a benchmark criterion tied to meeting the proficiency criterion on the year-end accountability measure indicates which students will likely fail the year-end measure without intervention. As a second example, if a benchmark criterion is used to reflect whether a child performs a skill in the frustration, instructional, or mastery range, the teacher can immediately identify which students are capable of more challenging work (i.e., those in the mastery range), which students are on track and gaining from instruction at that difficulty level (i.e., those in the instructional range), and which students are those for whom the work is too challenging (i.e., those in the frustration range). Combining a normative criterion with the benchmark is useful because it can allow for more efficient and targeted intervention services. For example, it is unlikely that children scoring higher than the 16th or 20th percentiles in a classroom would require intervention, even if they perform slightly below the benchmark criterion. We suggest that screening data be used to identify system-wide, grade-wide, and class-wide learning problems prior to identifying students for individual intervention.

RECOMMENDATIONS FOR INTERVENTION IMPLEMENTATION

Intervention Characteristics that Affect Decision Accuracy (Selection, Intensity, Implementation)

The RtI judgment is influenced by the degree to which a correct intervention was selected, the intensity of the intervention, and the integrity of intervention implementation. When these conditions are not met, the RtI judgment will likely be in error. Interventions should be selected on the basis of evidence that they have been effective when implemented for similar problems in the past (VanDerHeyden & Witt, 2008). Intervention selection should follow assessment of student performance such that the intervention is matched to a student's instructional level. Use of direct instruction protocols can effectively and efficiently promote rapid learning (Losardo & Bricker, 1994). Intervention protocols like those provided at www.gosbr.net, www.interventioncentral.org, and www.future-school-psychology.org may be of use to implementers. Such interventions emphasize use of materials for which the student can respond with a high degree of accuracy, modeling of correct responding, guided practice to respond with immediate corrective feedback, antecedent cues to signal and ensure correct responding, and timed intervals of brief practice with delayed feedback. Task difficulty is increased systematically as student learning improves, and generalization is assessed at routine intervals. Such interventions within RtI implementations have produced robust effects on learning with success rates of 90% RtI for those exposed to this type of intervention at Tier 3 (VanDerHeyden et al., 2007).

Empirically Supported Suggestions for Distinguishing Intervention Intensity

By definition, intervention intensity must increase across tiers. Many implementers have sought to define intervention intensity at each tier of RtI. Unfortunately, many of the suggested features for distinguishing intervention intensity (e.g., duration of intervention, frequency of intervention, session length, student to teacher ratio) are not necessarily associated with intensity. For example, one of the most common suggested characteristics to distinguish intervention intensity is duration of the intervention with longer duration interventions representing greater intensity. Whereas there is a good chance that longer duration interventions will produce stronger effects on learning, this need not necessarily be the case. A more reliable way to distinguish intervention intensity is the degree to which the intervention is individualized, how narrowly defined the target skills are, how gradually task difficulty is advanced during intervention, and whether intervention occurs for both skill establishment and generalization. We suggest that implementers focus on functional distinctions between tiers to ensure greater intensity as tiers progress. For example, interventions at Tier 2 that are delivered in a small-group or class-wide format might include a leaner schedule of feedback relative to a Tier 3 intervention, will likely advance task difficulty for the whole group simultaneously rather than at an individual student's pace of learning (as would happen at Tier 3), and might use group contingencies rather than an individualized contingency system.

Empirically Supported Procedures for Evaluating and Ensuring Adequate Intervention Implementation

Research suggests that correct intervention implementation requires strong antecedent support. Hence, implementers should: (a) ensure the intervention is acceptable to the teacher; (b) provide the teacher with a written protocol for implementation; and (c) train the teacher to implement the intervention with the student or students. The research is also clear that antecedent support, although necessary, is not sufficient. Research findings suggest that under optimal antecedent conditions, intervention implementation occurs correctly less than 20% of the time (Noell et al., 2005; Wickstrom, Jones, LaFleur, & Witt, 1998; Witt, Noell, LaFleur, & Mortenson, 1997). Hence, intervention follow-up, referred to as performance feedback, is necessary to ensure correct intervention implementation. Interventions should be reviewed for effects each week.

Where interventions are ineffective, intervention integrity should be assessed via direct observation of the intervention. Performance feedback should be delivered by a trained, competent, and diplomatic individual who knows how to implement the intervention (e.g., an intervention coach, a veteran teacher). This individual should provide the teacher with student learning data (intervention response) and intervention implementation data (the percentage of steps of the intervention implemented correctly, the percentage of days for which the intervention was conducted correctly), and should find out how the teacher can be better supported to implement the intervention correctly. Research is under way in this area to attempt to identify more efficient and scalable tools for monitoring and enhancing intervention implementation integrity. Potentially promising approaches include self-monitoring forms to report integrity (Sanetti & Kratochwill, 2009; Shapiro, 2009) at the initial stages and monitoring student learning data and providing integrity checks only where RtI is not sufficient (Gilbertson, Witt, Singletary, & VanDerHeyden, 2008). It is easy to imagine that technological applications may be used to enhance support provided to teachers via the Web. As research data emerge, new practices can and should be adopted.

RECOMMENDATIONS FOR EVALUATING RELIABILITY OF DECISIONS

Because RtI are gated decision models where (a) data are interpreted to reach a decision, (b) action follows accordingly, and (c) those data are interpreted in an iterative fashion, one major source of error is incorrect data interpretation. To facilitate reliable decision making at each stage, we recommend that software be used to organize the data and compute values on which the RtI judgment will be made. We suggest that decision rules and cut points be specified in advance. Finally, we recommend that implementers provide routine checks to ensure that the decisions correspond to the data and the decision rule.

RECOMMENDATIONS FOR EVALUATING STUDENT LEARNING OUTCOMES AT THE INDIVIDUAL, CLASSROOM, AND SYSTEM LEVEL TO ENSURE CONSEQUENTIAL VALIDITY OF EFFORTS

The exact assessment, intervention, and decision-making procedures may vary across RtI implementations. However, the effectiveness of RtI implementations can be evaluated so long as these criteria are met.

- The implementation details should be well specified. A good rule of thumb is that implementers should be able to describe what was done to reach the RtI decision such that an observer could replicate the activities to arrive at the same RtI judgment.
- Student learning data should be available by individual student and by demographic characteristics.
- Implementation data should be available to quantify the degree to which the RtI implementation occurred as planned. These data allow implementers to look at implementation effects, such as in the number of students at risk on consecutive screenings, the percentage of class-wide or grade-wide learning problems observed on consecutive screenings, and average level of student performance on screening measures and/or year-end accountability measures. Other indicators that might be important to the system include the number of children receiving Tier 2 and Tier 3 intervention, the percentage of children with a successful RtI, the percentage of children with an unsuccessful RtI, and the number of children evaluated and qualified for special education services. Demographic data can be used to examine each of these outcome indicators to evaluate proportionate effects.

⚓ TEST-YOURSELF QUESTIONS ⚓

1. There is no harm in evaluating a student for SLD when the parents and teachers wish for the child to be evaluated even when other data (e.g., RtI) suggest that evaluation is not needed.

   True or False?

2. Why are classification agreement analyses important to evaluating RtI effects?

3. Poor reading performance is a unique and specific marker for the presence of SLD in reading.

   True or False?

4. **Explain why poor reading performance is not unique to the condition of SLD.**

5. **Where base rates of a condition (e.g., SLD) are very low or very high, even very precise and accurate measures will likely be unimpressive in predicting the diagnosis.**

   True or False?

6. **Sensitivity is**

   (a) Computed as the number of test and criterion positives divided by the total number of criterion positives.

   (b) Determined via an index population.

   (c) Relatively unsusceptible to varying base rates.

   (d) The power of a test to detect true positives.

   (e) All of the above.

7. **Measures with high sensitivity when negative are useful for ruling in a disorder or condition.**

   True or False?

8. **Measures with high specificity when positive are useful for ruling in a disorder or condition.**

   True or False?

9. **Specificity**

   (a) Is the power of the test to detect true negatives.

   (b) Is highly dependent on the base rates of a condition.

   (c) Changes with each study.

   (d) Computed as the number of test negatives and criterion negatives divided by the total number of criterion negatives.

   (e) a and d.

10. **Positive and negative predictive power are highly dependent on base rates.**

    True or False?

11. **Define positive and negative predictive power.**

12. **Which indicator is useful in selecting a test to use for decision making?**

    (a) Sensitivity and specificity estimates.

    (b) Positive and negative predictive power.

    (c) Both a and b.

    (d) None of the above.

13. **Which indicator is most useful in interpreting an individual test finding?**

    (a) Sensitivity and specificity estimates.

    (b) Positive and negative predictive power.

    (c) Both a and b.

    (d) None of the above.

14. **Name several potential sources of error in an RtI decision.**

(continued)

Answers

1. False. Unnecessary evaluations carry the risk of a false positive identification error, the cost of the evaluation, and other costs related to the child and family's perspective on having a special education evaluation.
2. Because they can be used to quantify the accuracy of decisions made the cost of errors at each step and overall.
3. False
4. Because there are many potential causes of poor reading performance other than SLD including inadequate prior instruction and lack of motivation, for example.
5. True
6. e
7. False. Measures with high sensitivity when negative are useful for ruling out a disorder or condition.
8. True
9. e
10. True
11. Positive and negative predictive power estimates are referred to as diagnostic efficiency estimates because they provide an indication of a score or symptom's value in reaching a diagnosis. Positive predictive power is the probability that a positive test result is truly positive. Negative predictive power is the probability that a negative test result is truly negative.
12. a
13. b
14. See Table 3.1 for a list of potential sources of error and signs that these errors may have occurred.

Four

HOW TO INTERPRET RTI DATA

ontrary to popular belief, with the exception of readers of Wiley's "Essentials of" series, "data" does not have to be a four-letter word. Generally speaking, schools collect data on many issues and often have literally reams of data regarding individual students, classrooms, and school buildings. However, in our experience, school personnel generally do a poor job of consuming the data, and if the data are not consumed, then there is no reason to collect them. A good rule of thumb for schools to think about is if the data point does not lead to an actionable decision (e.g., change in instruction), then that data point should not be collected. Fortunately, No Child Left Behind has refocused school personnel on analyzing data to improve instruction, which in our opinion has been a positive outcome. However, school personnel are just now beginning to understand data and how to interpret the data we collect within an RtI model.

As stated in Chapter 1, the entire response to intervention (RtI) process can be conceptualized as a series of problem-analysis questions: (a) Which students require additional remediation? (all three tiers); (b) Is the problem specific to the student or the classroom? (Tier 1); (c) What is the category of the problem?

≡ Rapid Reference 4.1

RtI can be conceptualized as a series of problem-analysis questions:
- Which students require additional remediation? (all three tiers)
- Is the problem specific to the student or the classroom? (Tier 1)
- What is the category of the problem? (Tier 2)
- What is the causal variable? (Tier 3)
- Is the student making sufficient progress? (all three tiers)

(Tier 2); (d) What is the causal variable? (Tier 3), and (e) Is the student making sufficient progress? (all three tiers). This chapter discusses how to interpret RtI data in order to answer those questions.

WHICH STUDENTS REQUIRE ADDITIONAL REMEDIATION?

As consultants, we work closely with numerous school districts all across the country and frequently are asked exactly what school personnel should do to address a particular difficulty. Unfortunately, the answer we often give is to present several options and let the inquirer decide which would be best for the system in which he or she works. Each system is unique, and to pretend that we know what would be best would be misleading. Our answer often is met with some frustration, which we understand but cannot avoid. Readers are likely to feel that same frustration as they proceed through this section because identifying students who need additional remediation is the basic task of any RtI model, but there is no one best way to do so. Next we present two different approaches and arguments for and against each. The approach selected and implemented has to depend on the needs of the system, the priorities of the system, and what the system is able to implement well so that desired results can be attained.

Criterion-Referenced Approach

Student achievement data are interpreted in one of two ways. The data are interpreted either by comparing the student's obtained score to some meaningful cut score (e.g., a proficiency score on a state accountability test) or by determining the rank of the student's score to his or her peers. The former is referred to as criterion-referenced interpretation, and the latter is a norm-referenced interpretation (Anastasi & Urbina, 1997). Data obtained within an RtI framework are also interpreted with one of these two approaches or possibly a combination of the two.

A criterion-referenced approach has strong intuitive appeal because it compares student data to a meaningful criterion, and criterion-referenced approaches are especially useful for instructional decisions (Salvia, Ysseldyke, & Bolt, 2009). However, to what criterion should the data be compared? No Child Left Behind provides an answer to that critically important question. Students need to score in a proficient range on state accountability tests, which suggests that a proficient score on the state test could be the measure and criterion. However, many state tests are not administered until the spring of each school year, and students need to be identified as needing additional remediation much earlier in the year. Thus, many school districts are relying on alternative measures that can be given more frequently to predict who will and will not meet the proficiency criterion, such as the Measures of Academic Progress (MAP; Northwest Evaluation Association [NWEA], 2003) or curriculum-based measures of reading (CBM-R) and math (CBM-M).

Schools that use MAP data can simply employ standards reported by the NWEA because they are well established and linked to state and national tests. However, curriculum-based measures are the most frequently used assessment tools within an RtI framework (Gresham, 2002), and criteria are needed for those data. Suggested benchmarks are available for reading measures from the University of Oregon's Center on Teaching and Learning's (2008) Dynamic Indicators of Early Literacy Skills (DIBELS) Data System (https://dibels. uoregon.edu/benchmark.php). Practitioners can access easily used tables that group CBM-R data, collected three and four times per year for students through grade 6, into risk categories such as "some risk," "at risk," and "low risk." Although these classifications are easily and widely used, some have questioned decisions based on DIBELS classifications (Jenkins, Hudson, & Johnson, 2007; Kamii & Manning, 2005). Moreover, previous research found more accurate identification of struggling readers when interpretive criteria were derived from a local data set then when the DIBELS categories were used (Roehrig, Petscher, Nettles, Hudson, & Torgesen, 2008).

Given that school personnel need to be able to objectively identify struggling readers early in the school year but need proficiency on the state accountability test to serve as the criterion, individual cut scores could be developed based on CBM data and state test scores with a simple regression formula and spreadsheet software, such as Microsoft Excel. Most people are familiar with this basic regression equation:

$$Y = a + bX$$

where

Y = criterion being predicted (passing the state test score)
a = intercept of the two sets of data (the score on Y when X is 0)
b = slope of the line that intersects the two sets of data
X = independent variable (e.g., CBM-R score)

This equation can predict a student's score on the state test given his or her CBM-R score. However, we are interested in determining what CBM-R score predicts that the student would obtain a proficient score on the state test. In order

Table 4.1 Sample Data to Determine Cut Scores for Predicting State Test Proficiency

	A State Test Score	B Oral Reading Fluency (CBM-R)		A State Test Score	B Oral Reading Fluency (CBM-R)
1	191	108	18	189	90
2	177	56	19	191	44
3	179	22	20	184	58
4	179	85	21	176	24
5	196	89	22	209	122
6	199	46	23	196	90
7	184	54	24	193	54
8	201	90	25	209	131
9	175	21	26	189	36
10	223	159	27	192	105
11	174	32	28	198	89
12	179	56	29	203	149
13	188	131	30	201	166
14	205	144	31	202	23
15	187	55	32	185	63
16	188	141	33	200	125
17	210	66	34	196	39

to accomplish this, we need to know what cut score represents a proficient score (i.e., a passing score).

Consider the data in Table 4.1, which are presented in the same manner as data are entered into Excel.

Column A includes each student's state accountability test score, and column B is the CBM-R data recorded as words read correctly per minute. After the data are entered, we then need to know what test score equals proficiency for the state test. In this example of second-grade students, a score of 185 or higher is a proficient or passing score. Next, we use simple algebraic procedures to convert the previous equation, which is configured to determine Y (state test score), to determine X when Y = 185 (proficient score). The result of the algebraic conversion is presented next.

$$X = (vY - a)/b$$

In this example, Y = 185, but we still need "a" (intercept) and "b" (slope). Both of these values can be determined easily in Excel with the SLOPE and INTERCEPT functions, where the state test score is the dependent variable and the CBM-R score is the independent variable. To find the slope (b) and intercept (a), simply use the function wizard or enter "=SLOPE(A2:A35,B2:B35)" for slope and "INTERCEPT(A2:A35,B2:B35)" for intercept. The results are a slope of .16 and an intercept of 179.49. Thus, values for the previous equation are X = (185 [Y] – 179.49 [a])/.16 (b), which equals a score of 36.43 words read correctly per minute. Students who read at least 37 words correctly per minute likely will pass the state test. Five of the students in Table 4.1 read less than 37 words correct per minute, and all but one had a state test score of less than 185.

The calculations just demonstrated, and most criterion-referenced approaches, require cross-cohort comparisons because they involve a predictor (CBM-R score) and a criterion (state test score) that is completed at a different point in time. CBM-R data collected in the fall are used to predict the state test score that might not be taken until the spring, and we cannot wait until the spring to see if the CBM-R data suggest a problem. Therefore, we complete the analyses on a previous year's (or years') cohort (e.g., using the 2008–2009 third-grade data to determine CBM-R cut scores for 2009–2010 third graders). Cross-cohort comparisons are problematic because groups of students can be very different from year to year, but there is no other way to establish a criterion when it occurs later in the school year.

Another potential difficulty with a criterion-referenced approach to interpreting screening data is that it could result in 0% or 100% of the students being identified as requiring additional remediation, both of which would signal a significant flaw in the school's RtI model. On average, 20% of students need remediation beyond a quality core curriculum (Burns, Appleton, & Stehouwer, 2005), which aligns with recommendations that 20% of the student population receive a Tier 2 intervention (Batsche et al., 2005). Certainly high-performing schools could have close to 0% of the students who score below a criterion, but that would likely not identify students who could benefit from additional remediation. Moreover, a school that attempts to implement a Tier 2 intervention with over 20% of the student population likely will quickly exhaust its limited resources. Thus, it is perhaps most efficient to identify approximately 20% of the students as needing additional remediation through a Tier 2 intervention.

Norm-Referenced Approach

The alternative to a criterion-referenced approach would be to utilize a national or local norm to identify students who need a Tier 2 intervention in which the lowest 20% of all students would be identified as needing additional remediation. Several national norms are accessible to practitioners, including oral reading fluency norms available at http://readnaturally.com/howto/orftable. htm, and the national norms for several reading and math measures provided by Aimsweb (Pearson, 2008). The advantage of using a national norm provided by Aimsweb is that the data would represent the cohort from which the individual student belonged (e.g., a third grader would be compared to current third graders). The primary disadvantage is that it still would be possible for 0% or 100% of the students to be identified as needing a Tier 2 intervention. Thus, using a national norm does not provide the primary benefit of using a normative approach: providing assistance to a set number of students determined by some normative criterion.

Local norms are frequently associated with CBMs because they can indicate typical performance that may assist in screening and goal setting (Kaminski & Good, 1999; Shinn, 1987; Stewart & Silberglitt, 2008). A local norm interpretation of RtI data involves collecting data for all students through universal screening and providing a Tier 2 intervention for the lowest 20% of the student population. The 20% rule is dependent on school resources; that number could go up if resources allow. A particular advantage of a local norming approach is the ease of interpretation and the fact that the process can be applied to any set of data for which universal screening is conducted. Moreover, RtI primarily involves the use of assessment data to allocate resources efficiently (Burns & VanDerHeyden, 2006; Tilly, 2008), and local norms can facilitate resource allocation.

Within a local norming approach to identifying struggling learners, Tier 2 interventions are provided for the lowest 20% of the student population, regardless of the actual score. In other words, it is possible that students identified as needing additional remediation could read proficiently, and it is theoretically possible that students who do not read proficiently are not identified. Further, it is highly possible that a child would be eligible to receive intervention in one school context but ineligible in another, much like the existing model of specific learning disability (SLD) service delivery. Within an RtI model, the resources are allocated to the students who need them the most, which means that even in a high-performing school where students consistently meet or exceed state and national standards, the lowest-scoring students receive additional support to enhance their learning.

Although we stated that theoretically not every student who is a struggling learner could be identified as needing additional support based on local norms, a model in which that actually occurred would be significantly flawed. Local norms are useful for identifying students for remediation only if class-wide problems do not exist or are successfully alleviated. We will talk about determining class-wide problems later, but consider the data in Table 4.1 as an example. If we use a normative approach, then 4 of the 20 students (20%) would be identified as needing a Tier 2 intervention. The fall universal screening occurred on September 15 and indicated that any student reading 12 or fewer words correctly per minute (wcpm) would need additional academic support. However, the 25th percentile nationally for second graders in the fall is 25 wcpm (Hasbrouck & Tindal, 1987), and any student reading less than 25 wcpm is considered to be at risk for reading difficulties according to the DIBELS classifications (Center for Teaching and Learning, 2008). Thus, there appear to be 12 out of 20 (60%) students who could be considered to be struggling readers, 8 (40%) of whom will not receive an intervention. These data point out the need for first addressing a class-wide problem because after doing so (September 29 data), the lowest 20% received scores of 13 wcpm or less and *no* students read between 13 and 25 wcpm. In this example, all of the students who required an intervention received one. Chapter 2 discussed class-wide interventions (and how we obtained these positive results), and we discuss how to identify a class-wide problem next.

> ### CAUTION
> Class-wide learning problems should be addressed using class-wide intervention before applying a local normative criterion to determine individual student risk.

CLASS-WIDE PROBLEMS

The data in Table 4.2 show the need for a class-wide intervention but also demonstrate the effectiveness of the intervention. The class median more than doubled from 19.5 to 45.5 in just 2 weeks among these second graders attending an urban school in Minnesota. Previous research consistently demonstrated both the effectiveness of class-wide interventions (VanDerHeyden & Burns, 2005; VanDerHeyden, Witt, & Naquin, 2003) and the need for them; VanDerHeyden

Table 4.2 Sample Oral Reading Fluency Data for a Class of Second-Grade Students

Student	September 15	September 29	Winter	Spring
A	11	12	12	27
B	16	33	51	71
C	12	28	41	62
D	29	45	71	76
E	23	46	60	74
F	34	52	76	86
G	14	27	40	55
H	13	13	16	18
I	13	26	29	71
J	30	59	88	105
K	31	59	64	81
L	13	29	45	61
M	10	12	14	38
N	37	50	70	75
O	31	56	81	71
P	9	13	17	13
Q	33	54	74	90
R	20	46	72	76
S	40	62	86	95
T	19	47	52	82
Median	19.5	45.5	56	72.5

and Burns (2005) found class-wide problems in every classroom in the participating elementary school.

The first step in interpreting the data within an RtI model should be to examine them according to classrooms. Thus, after the universal screening data are collected, they are arranged by classroom teacher and the class median is reported. The reason we use class median (instead of an average) is that the presence of one or two outliers in a small data set—and, statistically speaking, a set of fewer than 30 is small—can affect the average dramatically. The class median is then compared to some criterion but *not* a local norm. Determining whether a class-wide learning problem exists needs to be a criterion-based decision because we are trying to detect the presence of a difficulty rather than allocating resources, and it is acceptable to have 0% or 100% of the classrooms identified as having a class-wide problem at this stage of decision making.

≡ Rapid Reference 4.2

First steps in an RtI model:

1. Report class medians for universal screening data.
2. Compare the class median to the 25th percentile from national norms or to a criterion (e.g., instructional level for the grade group or empirically derived criterion).
3. Identify class-wide problems if the class median is below the criterion, and implement a class-wide intervention.

Three options to which data can be compared are national norms, empirically derived criteria, and instructional-level criteria. The national norms described earlier can also serve as a criterion for class-wide problem identification. When using a national norm, it is best to compare the class median to the 25th percentile for that grade and time of year. For example, the data presented in Table 4.2 have a class median of 19.5, which is below the 25th percentile for second graders in the fall of 25 wcpm. The 25th percentile is used because it represents the lowest end of the average range and is a frequently used criterion for identifying struggling learners (e.g., Torgesen et al., 2001).

Using national norms is probably the easiest option for school personnel to identify class-wide problems. However, school personnel could use the regression formula presented earlier to identify the CBM score that predicts a proficient score on a state test and use that as the criterion. Alternatively, a district could also conduct a receiver operating characteristics curve[*] analysis, which is a more advanced way to determine which score predicts a passing score on the state test. The resulting criteria would have the advantage of being local and directly linked to accountability tests, and could be computed with any data with which students are universally screened. Although these options are relatively simple analyses, personnel trained in statistical methodologies

---

[*]For further ROC information, see the Authors' Note beginning on page 146.

(e.g., a research and evaluation department or director) are required to conduct these analyses. If no such person can be found within the school district, then national norms or instructional level criteria can be used.

As stated, VanDerHeyden and colleagues have demonstrated the importance of identifying a class-wide problem and the effectiveness of class-wide interventions (VanDerHeyden & Burns, 2005; VanDerHeyden et al., 2003). Although we present three options here, VanDerHeyden and her colleagues use instructional-level criteria to determine if there is a class-wide problem. The concept of an instructional level was first articulated by Betts (1946). It represents a level of material for which the student can respond successfully but also contains enough new material to be challenging (Gravois & Gickling, 2008). The Gickling and Thompson (1985) instructional level criterion of 93% to 97% known words within reading is well researched but has not been used to identify class-wide problems because few classrooms would result in a median of less than 93% known words. Instead, the Deno and Mirkin (1977) criteria of 40 to 60 words correct/minute (first and second grade) and 70 to 100 words correct/minute (third to sixth grade) have been used to identify class-wide problems. However, it should be noted that the Deno and Mirkin criteria were derived from experience in one school in Minnesota (S. L. Deno, personal communication, April 15, 2005), which suggests limited utility in other districts across the country. Math data can be interpreted with instructional level criteria of 14 to 31 digits correct per minute (dcpm) for second and third graders and 24 to 49 dcpm for fourth and fifth graders (Burns, VanDerHeyden, & Jiban, 2006). Of course, the math instructional-level criteria were not researched with older students; there do not seem to be acceptable criteria for students beyond fifth grade.

CATEGORY OF DIFFICULTY

After class-wide problems are remediated and students are identified as needing a Tier 2 intervention, we must determine which intervention would be most appropriate. Approximately 15% to 20% of students will receive a Tier 2 intervention, which suggests that only low-level problem analyses are possible. Thus, our goal in Tier 2 is to identify the category of the problem based on assessments of specific skills.

For reading, assessments are conducted within the five areas of the National Reading Panel (NRP, 2000): phonemic awareness, phonics, reading fluency, vocabulary, and comprehension. Math data focus on the sequence of skills within a curriculum (e.g., single-digit multiplication, then single-digit division, then multidigit multiplication, etc.). Once the data are collected, we compare them to instructional-level criteria (described earlier) to find the highest-level skill in which an instructional level can be achieved, and intervention begins there.

Reading is treated sequentially in that phonemic awareness generally precedes phonetics, which generally precedes fluent reading, which generally leads to better vocabulary and comprehension (Adams, 1990; Berninger, Abbott, Vermeulen, & Fulton, 2006; Chall, 1983; Snow, Burns, & Griffin, 1998). However, the criteria for an instructional level are limited to oral reading fluency and cannot be used to evaluate phonics, phonemic awareness, or comprehension. Thus, the "some risk" criterion from the DIBELS standards (Center for Teaching and Learning, 2008) can be used for those skills.

CAUSAL VARIABLE

On average, 5% of the student body will require intensive interventions beyond Tier 2 (Burns et al., 2005), and a Tier 3 intervention is implemented. As stated in Chapter 1, the problem analysis approach (Heartland Area Education Agency, 2002) is used frequently to identify the malleable variables that contribute to a problem (i.e., casual variable). Heartland Area Education Agency refers to the problem analysis process as collecting relevant information on the instruction, curriculum, environment, and learner (ICEL) using reviews, interviews, observations, and tests (RIOT). Additional intervention heuristics could be used (e.g., Burns, Christ, Boice, & Szadokierski, in press; Daly, Chafouleas, & Skinner, 2004; Haring & Eaton, 1978), but explaining them in any detail is beyond the scope of this book. However, these heuristics involve assessing individual skills and evaluating the rate (i.e., speed with which the skill can be completed successfully) and accuracy with which they are completed.

For example, the Learning Hierarchy (Haring & Eaton, 1978) proposes that students progress through four phases when learning a new skill: acquisition, proficiency, generalization, and adaptation. When students first learn a skill, they are slow and inaccurate and the learner is said to be at the Acquisition Phase in learning that skill. After initial instruction, students complete the skill more accurately but remain dysfluent because their responses are slow and hesitant. This stage is referred to as the Fluency Phase. During the next phase, the Generalization Phase, students can quickly and accurately perform the skill under contexts and conditions that are similar to training but also begin to use the skill when exposed to novel materials and contexts. Finally, students apply the newly learned skill to solve problems, which is the Adaptation Phase. Thus, students in the Acquisition Phase require interventions that focus on building response accuracy, and those in the Fluency Phase require interventions that increase the rate of accurate skill performance. Students in the latter two stages require different instructional strategies, such as problem solving, discrimination/differentiation training, and practice to apply mastered skills under novel conditions and to solve more complex tasks (Burns, VanDerHeyden, & Jiban, 2006). Research has consistently demonstrated that the Learning Hierarchy is an effective intervention heuristic (Ardoin & Daly, 2007).

We have discussed evaluating the rate of the skill repeatedly but have yet to give attention to accuracy. The rate at which students complete a task can be evaluated with instructional-level criteria or with national norms (i.e., scoring at or above the 25th percentile). Accuracy can also be evaluated with instructional-level criteria using the percentage of the items correctly completed. Gickling and Thompson (1985) proposed that students should be able to read correctly 93% to 97% of the words in a passage for that passage to represent instructional-level difficulty. Use of 93% to 97% known material has been supported consistently with research (Burns, 2007; Gickling & Armstrong, 1978; Treptow, Burns, & McComas, 2007). Thus, for reading fluency, a second grader reading 10 wcpm with 85% known words would be both slow and inaccurate (Acquisition Phase) and would likely require modeling of the skill, but a student who read 10 wcpm with 95% known words (Fluency Phase) would likely benefit from additional practice, such as repeated reading, with contingencies for faster but still accurate performance.

Math and most skills other than reading for comprehension can be evaluated as drill tasks (Gickling, 1984). Meta-analytic research found that 90% known led to the largest average effects within drill tasks (Burns, 2004). Thus, 90% is probably the most appropriate accuracy criterion for academic areas such as multiplication facts, letter sounds, comprehension questions, and just about any skill other than reading fluency.

PROGRESS MONITORING

School personnel monitor student progress throughout all three intervention tiers. In fact, how much a student has improved is perhaps the most important piece of information to a classroom teacher or a student's parents. Student progress in an RtI model typically is assessed in terms of their level and rate of achievement (Gresham, 2002). The two most common approaches to evaluate student growth data are aimlines and dual discrepancies (DD), both of which are discussed next.

Aimline

An aimline is the expected rate of progress in order for student response to be evaluated positively and is graphically depicted by drawing a line that connects the initial level of performance and the desired level at the goal date. Student data are plotted in a time-series graph, and progress is measured by comparing subsequent data points to the aimline. Data points that approximate the aimline suggest that the student is making sufficient progress. Three consecutive data points above the aimline suggest that a more ambitious goal is needed, and three consecutive data points below the aimline suggest that the intervention is not effective (Fuchs, Fuchs, Hintze, & Lembke, 2006; Mirkin, Deno, Tindal, & Kuehnle, 1982; Shinn, 1989). In an RtI model, three consecutive data points below the aimline could suggest that the intervention is not intense enough and a change in tier may be needed (Fuchs et al., 2006).

Previous research found that using aimlines and graphing student data resulted in more frequent revisions to student education plans and increased student achievement (Fuchs, Fuchs, Hamlett, & Stecker, 1991). However, aimlines can be problematic for some decisions because similar growth rates for different students could result in different decisions based on the level of baseline performance or time allowed (VanDerHeyden, Witt, & Barnett, 2005). For example, a student who read 30 wcpm may have 30 weeks to obtain a year-end goal of 60 wcpm, which would be a rate of growth of 2 wcpm per week. However, a student who started at 15 wcpm would have to increase by 1.5 wcpm per week to approximate the aimline, and a student who started at 30 wcpm but had only 10 weeks to make the goal would have to increase by 3 wcpm per week. Moreover, recent research has questioned the reliability of decisions made by comparing rates of growth to aimlines (Burns, Scholin, Kosciolek, & Livingston, in press; VanDerHeyden, Witt, & Barnett, 2005).

Dual Discrepancy

Instead of making decisions with comparisons to aimlines within graphs of student data, it might be more psychometrically sound to use a dual discrepancy (DD) approach. Previous research found that using both rate of growth and level of the skill led to better decisions than either one alone (Fuchs, 2003) and decisions made with a dual discrepancy framework were more reliable than those using an aimline (Burns et al., in press). Moreover, using dual discrepancy criteria for identification of struggling learners converged with the outcomes of norm-referenced reading tests (Burns & Senesac, 2005; McMaster, Fuchs, Fuchs, &

Compton, 2005; Speece & Case, 2001; Speece, Case, & Molloy, 2003) and differentiated reading skills from at-risk students who did not exhibit a dual discrepancy (Burns & Senesac, 2005).

Both level and rate of growth are evaluated within a dual discrepancy model using CBMs. Post-intervention level usually is evaluated with criterion-referenced approaches, such as scoring above the 25th percentile on a national norm or scoring within the low-risk category from the DIBELS standards. Rate of growth is calculated numerically and evaluated through a local normative approach, such as placing at or above the 25th percentile for a particular grade or scoring within 1 standard deviation of the average rate of growth for one grade.

Slopes of growth can be computed with Excel by entering CBM data and weeks within respective columns as shown in Table 4.3. The data included in the table are from benchmark assessments, but the process is the same regardless of the timeframe. First, the data are entered in rows for each student (cells A, B, and C), then the number of the week for the school year is entered into the next columns (cells D, E, and F in Table 4.3). The number of data points and number of weeks should be identical (e.g., 3 and 3). It is important to use the number representing the week of the school year. For example, the data in Table 4.3 were collected during the first week of the school year, the 17th week of the school year, and the 33rd week of the school year. The numbers 1, 17, and 33 could be entered only once in cells D2, E2, and F2 and then dragged into subsequent boxes. Next, the slope function can be used to determine the numeric rate of growth or by entering =SLOPE(A2:C2,D2:F2) into cell G, which then can be dragged into the remaining rows. Thus, once the data are entered, the slope of growth for a very large set of data can be computed in approximately 5 minutes.

The mean rate of growth for the data presented in Table 4.3 is 1.48 wcpm per week and the standard deviation is .86 wcpm per week. Thus, using a dual discrepancy approach, a student who scored within 1 standard deviation of the mean (.62 wcpm per week or higher) or who scored above the 25th percentile (.70 wcpm per week in Table 4.2) would be making satisfactory progress. It should be noted that data are presented for only 23 students in Table 4.3, but making normative decisions with such a small data set could be problematic. Thus, grade level rather than classroom is used to compute average slopes of growth. For example in a school with three classrooms per grade, there may be only 25 third graders in each class, but there would be 75 total third-grade students, which would be a data set that is large enough to analyze. In schools with only one classroom per grade or even fewer, data are compiled across grade groupings.

After slopes of growth are computed and evaluated, the information is coupled with the level data and student growth is evaluated. A student who

Table 4.3 Sample Slope of Growth Data

	A	B	C	D	E	F	G
	Fall	Winter	Spring	Week of Fall Benchmark	Week of Winter Benchmark	Week of Spring Benchmark	Slope
1	26	29	79	1	17	33	1.66
2	43	55	108	1	17	33	2.03
3	57	60	84	1	17	33	0.84
4	53	55	89	1	17	33	1.13
5	66	93	166	1	17	33	3.13
6	59	67	73	1	17	33	0.44
7	26	42	92	1	17	33	2.06
8	64	77	112	1	17	33	1.50
9	36	30	58	1	17	33	0.69
10	23	28	59	1	17	33	1.13
11	40	64	112	1	17	33	2.25
12	28	34	34	1	17	33	0.19
13	6	22	42	1	17	33	1.13
14	45	43	64	1	17	33	0.59
15	51	61	136	1	17	33	2.66
16	43	56	77	1	17	33	1.06
17	89	112	169	1	17	33	2.50
18	31	40	89	1	17	33	1.81
19	29	56	132	1	17	33	3.22
20	64	78	116	1	17	33	1.63
21	37	54	60	1	17	33	0.72
22	31	31	48	1	17	33	0.53
23	48	50	87	1	17	33	1.22

scores below a criterion for post-intervention level (e.g., scoring in the at-risk range on DIBELS criteria) and whose slope of growth was more than 1 standard deviation below the mean (e.g., less than .62 in Table 4.2) would be exhibiting a dual discrepancy. In this case both the post-intervention fluency and rate of growth are low, and the intervention would be judged as ineffective. It may also be possible to consider using an intervention within a more intensive tier (e.g., from Tier 2 to Tier 3). If a student's rate of growth is low (e.g., less than .62 in Table 4.2) but his or her level is above a criterion (e.g., within the low-risk DIBELS category), then the student is not exhibiting a dual discrepancy, and change in intervention is not warranted. For example, a student who scores very high on the fall benchmark might not grow as much as many students because of a ceiling effect. A classroom teacher would carefully consider these data for that student and attempt to provide a more challenging experience, but from an RtI perspective, a change in tier is not warranted. Conversely, a student might score quite low before and after an intervention was attempted but make large gains in the process. For example, a second-grade student might read 5 wcpm in September and increase to 65 wcpm in May. The DIBELS standard for at-risk is 25 wcpm in the fall and 69 in the spring. Thus, the student fell within the at-risk category for both fall and spring assessments but increased by 60 words during the 30 weeks between the two. Thus, he increased by 2.0 wcpm per week, which is probably above the grade-level mean and above standards associated with effective practice (e.g., 1.39 wcpm per week; Deno et al., 1977). This student started low and ended low but significantly closed the gap. Thus, this student's progress would be judged as adequate, and the intervention and intervention tier would continue.

As with local normative interpretations of student data, determining the average slope of growth necessitates cross-cohort comparisons. Because of the concerns about comparing groups of students, Silberglitt and Gibbons (2005) developed a norm-referenced approach to evaluate level and a criterion approach for slope of growth. In this model, a student's CBM-R post-intervention level is considered below expectations if it falls below the seventh percentile on local norms. Targets for rates of growth were computed by determining the scores that predict passing the state test at the three benchmark assessments. Using a process similar to the one just described, target benchmark scores were derived to predict a proficient score on the state test. Next, the rate of growth necessary to obtain those scores is computed. For example, oral reading fluency scores that predict a proficient score on the state test for fourth-grade students are 83 in the fall, 101 in the winter, and 113 in the spring. The slope of growth for those three data points is .83 wcpm per week (Burns & Gibbons, 2008). Finally, student data are considered dually discrepant if the CBM score falls below the seventh percentile on the local norm and the slope of growth is below .83 in fourth grade (Silberglitt & Gibbons, 2005).

A Note about Slopes

Deno's seminal work (1986, 2002; Deno & Mirkin, 1977) established the instructional utility of slopes of learning and comparing those slopes to criteria such as aimlines. We enthusiastically support slope data to inform instruction, but research has yet to fully validate important decisions (i.e., SLD identification) based on slope data, and standards for educational and psychological assessment require that all purposes for which data are used be validated for each purpose (American Educational Research Association, American Psychological Association, National Council for Measurement in Education, 1999). Certainly some preliminary work support diagnostic decisions based on dual discrepancies that partially rely on slope data (Burns & Senesac, 2005; Fuchs, 2003; Speece & Case, 2001; Speece et al., 2003), but practitioners should exercise caution when interpreting numeric slopes (Schatschneider, Wagner, & Crawford, 2008). (See Chapter 3 for more information.)

SLD is a meaningless construct without assessing learning (Fletcher, personal communication, 2008). Thus, slope data can be used to inform diagnostic decisions, but only if the data are collected with proper administration procedures that include well-constructed assessment probes. Moreover, sufficient data are needed for slopes to be reliable. According to Christ (2006), approximately eight data points are needed, assuming adequate assessment procedures, in order for the data to be sufficiently reliable for decisions. In our opinion, slope data are best used to identify a positive response, such as when a student makes large gains but remains below a proficiency level or when the

CAUTION

Slope data should be used cautiously!

- Slopes are indicators of intervention effectiveness and are not validated for diagnostic decision making.
- Slope data must be collected with proper administration procedures that use well-constructed probes.
- At least eight data points are needed for reliable decision making.
- Slope data are best interpreted when they agree with level estimates.

data agree with level data (i.e., both indicate a need for change or a successful intervention). However, if level and slope data conflict (e.g., slope indicates a need for change but level does not, or vice versa), then practitioners should consider giving preference to level. For example, if slope data suggest that the student has made sufficient progress but the student remains below the level associated with proficiency, then the intervention would continue.

SUMMARY

Data are the key to effective instruction and intervention in K–12 schools. In fact, the terms "RtI," "assessment," and "data-based decision making" are synonymous. RtI came out of special education regulations, and "special education" is defined as "specialized instruction, at no cost to the parents or guardians, to meet the unique needs of a child with a disability" (IDEA, P.L. 108–446). The only way to deliver special education is to determine the unique needs of a child, and the only way to determine unique needs is assessment. Assessment is necessary not only for special education but also for education that is special.

Although research is still needed, we have recently learned a great deal about data-based decision making in schools. Empirical inquiry suggested the need to identify class-wide problems by comparing class medians to a criterion-referenced standard, to target interventions based on data, and to monitor progress frequently. However, comparing student progress to an aimline in order to make important decisions (e.g., tiered intervention placement and special education eligibility) seems to be a questionable practice. Dual discrepancies are the more psychometrically sound approach, but slope data also should be carefully interpreted.

> **DON'T FORGET**
> ....
> Assessment is defined as a process by which data are used to make decisions (Anastasi & Urbina, 1997; Salvia et al., 2007), which suggests that unless data are used to make decisions, assessment is not occurring, regardless of how often students are tested.

Most schools recognize the importance of assessment but usually respond by engaging in frequent testing of student skills. Assessment is defined as a process by which data are used to make decisions (Anastasi & Urbina, 1997; Salvia et al., 2007), which suggests that unless data are used to make decisions, assessment is not occurring, regardless of how often students are tested. We have discussed the decisions typically made in an RtI framework and how to interpret the data to make them. Remember that, with data, anything is possible, as long as school personnel consume the data in an objective and standardized manner.

🦅 TEST-YOURSELF QUESTIONS 🦅

1. **All data points collected should lead to an actionable decision or should not be collected.**

   True or False?

2. **Criterion-referenced decision rules compare student performance to some criterion that is predictive of success. What is the downside to use of criterion-referenced decision rules in RtI?**

3. **Norm-referenced decision rules use a normative criterion to identify students at risk (e.g., all students performing below the 25th percentile at universal screening). What is the downside to using norm-referenced decision rules in RtI?**

4. **What are the two most common ways to evaluate student progress in RtI?**

5. **The rate of growth required to surpass an aimline criterion is dependent on the baseline starting level of performance and the amount of time allocated to the intervention trial.**

   True or False?

6. **A dual discrepancy is signified by a rate of growth during intervention that is lower than the rate of growth of students who are not at risk.**

   True or False?

7. **True or False. A slope can be reliably computed given three data points.**

   True or False?

Answers

1. True.
2. The downside is that if all students perform above criterion, then no specialized resources will be allocated for a school to support those who are low-performing relative to their peers.
3. Children who are at-risk academically may not appear in the norm-referenced risk group (e.g., the bottom 25%) and therefore would not receive intervention even though they may be predicted to fail without intervention.
4. Aimline and dual discrepancy criterion.
5. True.
6. False. A dual discrepancy is indicated by both a lower rate of growth and a lower level of performance following intervention.
7. False. Recent data suggest that reliable estimation of slope is technically challenging. Findings suggest that at least eight data points are needed to reliably estimate slope. Additional research is needed on this topic to tease out the parameters of slope measurement that affect decision accuracy.

Five

EVALUATING THE RESEARCH BASE FOR RTI

R esponse to intervention (RtI) is perhaps the most substantial reform in education and special education since the initial authorization of the Elementary and Secondary Education Act in 1965. It has been endorsed by several professional associations, implemented in some form in all 50 states, and is a frequent topic for presentations at state and national conferences. The energy and buzz around RtI have not been seen in quite some time. It is not surprising that educators are either enthusiastic or passionately skeptical about RtI because the field tends to move in one of those two directions whenever a new innovation occurs. As Ellis (2005) states, educators are continuously searching for new and better methods to improve children's education. Unfortunately, as Ellis also points out, this fanfare and fascination with what is new often fulfills the 17th-century Spanish writer Baltasar Gracian y Morales's caution that "brand-new mediocrity is thought more of than accustomed excellence." However, schools often widely adopt the new mediocrity without asking critical questions, such as: Is it effective? Will it work in my school? What is necessary to implement it successfully? After those questions are answered, the supposed innovation falls out of favor as quickly as it emerged.

Ellis (2005) proposed that educational initiatives should be evaluated through research at three different levels. Research should address a sound theoretical base (Level I), demonstrated effectiveness (Level II), and effectiveness of implementation on a wide-scale basis (Level III). Innovations that are implemented on a large scale but that lack a sound theoretical base and/or researched effectiveness are educational fads that come and go. Innovations based on sound theory and research may not impact education if they are not consistently implemented or do not find their way into many classrooms. In this chapter we review RtI research regarding the three levels of research proposed by Ellis and discuss the strengths and weaknesses of RtI within each.

LEVEL I: SOUND THEORETICAL BASIS

The goal of Level I research is to establish the validity of a theoretical construct or idea developed from basic research or from a philosophical perspective. Although several theories and philosophical perspectives influence RtI, the most direct and influential perspectives seem to be prevention science and problem solving.

Prevention Science

Prevention science is the process of identifying potential risk and protective factors in order to eliminate or mitigate major human dysfunction (Coie et al., 1993). Research has consistently demonstrated the effectiveness of prevention efforts (Botvin, 2004; Greenberg, Domitrovich, & Bumbarger, 1999; Stith et al., 2006; Wilson, Gottfredson, & Najaka, 2001), and prevention science has influenced several fields including counseling psychology (Hage et al., 2007) and public health (Nussbaum, 2006). The major human dysfunction that RtI attempts to prevent is learning difficulties and specific learning disabilities (SLD). Rapid Reference 5.1 lists the principles of prevention science (Coie et al., 1993) and how RtI addresses each one.

≣ *Rapid Reference 5.1*

Principles of Prevention Science

- Address fundamental causal factors.
- Address risk factors before they stabilize.
- Target those at high risk.
- Coordinate action in each domain of functioning.

Address Fundamental Causal Factors

Decades of research have attempted to identify the causal factors for SLD and have consistently demonstrated very few differences between students identified as SLD and garden-variety low achievers (Aaron, 1997; Greenberg, Ehri, & Pehrin, 1997; Lyon, 1995; Siegel, 1993; Stanovich & Siegel, 1994). However, a lack of phonological awareness (Greenberg et al., 1997) and poor reading instruction (Foorman, Francis, & Fletcher, 1998) have both been shown to lead directly to diagnosed learning disabilities. Thus, quality instruction that addresses the core aspects of learning is an important target for the prevention of SLD, and research has consistently demonstrated its effectiveness in doing so (Lennon & Slesinski, 1999; Torgesen, Rose, Lindamood, Conway, & Garvan, 1999; Torgesen et al., 2001).

RtI directly addresses the causal factors by emphasizing a quality core curriculum and by targeting learning deficits through specific interventions. Repeatedly throughout this book we have discussed the importance of identifying class-wide problems as the first step to an RtI model, because without a quality core curriculum, nothing else matters. One of the core characteristics of an RtI model is that it is based on low-inference decisions in which the behaviors can be directly observed and data are used to identify the need for interventions, select interventions, and evaluate the effects of those interventions (Christ, 2006). Thus, a student who needs remediation with reading fluency will receive a fluency intervention (e.g., repeated reading), and progress will be monitored with oral reading fluency.

> # DON'T FORGET
> ....
> Use of RtI has resulted in lower rates of SLD, improved proportionality or indicators of equity, earlier delivery of special education services, and increased student achievement.

Previous RtI research found lower rates of SLD in schools that implemented RtI (Burns, Appleton, & Stehouwer, 2005), and the rates of SLD within a school went down after RtI was implemented (Sornson, Frost, & Burns, 2005; Van-DerHeyden, Witt, & Gilbertson, 2007). Descriptive research found that the rate of SLD remained stable after implementation (decrease by 3.8%), but disproportionality in special education decreased, special education services were provided at younger ages, and student achievement increased (Marston, Muyskens, Lau, & Canter, 2003). Although these studies did not examine what aspect of RtI led to these effects, which could be an area for future research, the effects were clear.

Address Risk Factors before They Stabilize

One of the basic assumptions of RtI is that it uses a risk model in which learning and behavioral difficulties are identified early (Gresham, 2007). The term "early" here is used two ways. First, it is in reference to the universal screening conducted within RtI. All RtI models attempt to identify a difficulty well before it becomes severe enough to warrant special education consideration. Even RtI's most skeptical critics acknowledge that RtI can prevent difficulties through early intervention (Batsche, Kavale, & Kovaleski, 2006; Reynolds & Shaywitz, 2009b). Second, RtI focuses on younger children than does traditional special education.

The rates of students receiving special education services among 6- to 11-year-olds in 2004 was approximately 4% of the student population, but that number jumped to over 6% for students ages 12 to 17 years (U.S. Department of Education, 2009). This increase is somewhat concerning because the rates should decline due to effective treatment, and interventions have a higher likelihood of success the earlier they are implemented. Most RtI models focus on elementary schools and on early elementary grades, which is consistent with prevention science but suggests that additional research is needed for students in middle and high schools.

Target Those at High Risk

RtI utilizes tiers of intervention that match student need to intervention intensity. In fact, the three-tiered model so frequently used within RtI can be linked back directly to public health and prevention efforts (Ervin, Schaughency, Goodman, McGlinchey, & Matthews, 2007; Sugai & Horner, 2006). RtI is the practice of allocating resources based on student needs, and many schools triage students into the three tiers based on universal screening data. Although triaging is a practice for which there is no research base, we suggest that it is consistent with the prevention science principle of targeting those at risk.

It is unlikely that universal screening data could be used to accurately triage to varying degrees of intervention intensity. But it is very possible to very accurately and efficiently make these types of triage decisions following brief iterative assessments (see Chapter 3). By analogy, when a sick patient arrives in an emergency department for evaluation, the treating physician makes a triage decision followed by assessment, brief treatment, and more assessment before making a second triage-type judgment, and so on. This iterative triaging is what occurs with and what is supported in RtI implementations.

CAUTION

It is critical that RtI align with the prevention science principle of coordinated action, but how well coordination actually happens and the breadth of the coordination are matters of some debate and are areas for future research.

Coordinate Action in Each Domain of Functioning

During a recent workshop one of the authors was asked by a classroom teacher: "How will my life be different if we do RtI?" The answer was that it will be different in two ways:

1. Teachers will use objective data much more frequently to make decisions.
2. There will be more professionals in the classroom.

In order for RtI to be effective, it has to be "all hands on deck" (Kysar, 2009) in which special education, general education, Title 1, and other areas all merge resources to address the needs of all children. Every RtI advocate discusses the importance of collaborating within the school, but few talk about coordinating with other agencies. Moreover, it is unknown how well coordination occurs within schools. Thus, it is critical that RtI align with the prevention science principle of coordinated action. How well it actually happens at this time and the breadth of the coordination are matters of some debate and are areas for future research.

Problem Solving

As stated in Chapter 1, the roots of RtI trace directly back to the University of Minnesota's Institute of Research on Learning Disabilities (IRLD) and the *Data-Based Program Modification* manual (Mirkin et al., 1982). The work started by the IRLD quickly evolved into a problem-solving framework (Deno, 2002) based on the IDEAL (Identify, Define, Explore, Apply, and Look) (Bransford & Stein, 1984) model of:

1. Identify the problem.
2. Define the problem.
3. Explore alternative solutions to the problem.
4. Apply a solution.
5. Look at the effects of the application.

These steps in the problem-solving model can be core components of any RtI model (Burns, Deno & Jimerson, 2007). A description of how RtI models address these core components follows.

1. Identify the Problem

General outcome measures, such as curriculum-based measurement (CBM), are especially useful in identifying areas of skill deficits for children, and CBM has been identified as an essential component of any RtI model (Burns, Dean, & Klar, 2004; Burns & Ysseldyke, 2005; Gresham, 2002). Data obtained from brief assessments of academic skills for all students can be used to identify children with potential difficulties. Thus, the first step of the problem-solving process is to screen the academic skills of all students, called universal screening. Research is beginning to identify the effectiveness of using screening data to enhance the learning outcomes of all children (Ardoin et al., 2004; Glover & Albers, 2007; VanDerHeyden, Witt, & Naquin 2003).

2. Define the Problem

Clearly and explicitly defining the problem is the "key to success" of problem-solving (Deno, 2002, p. 46), but few RtI models convey steps to defining the problem. The Screening to Enhance Educational Progress (STEEP; VanDer-Heyden et al., 2003) begins this process by first examining if the difficulty is specific to the child or the classroom of children and by then determining if the deficit is primarily due to a lack of skill or of motivation (Ardoin et al., 2004; VanDerHeyden et al., 2003). Other approaches to defining the problem usually involve comparing the child's rate of progress to a projected rate of growth necessary to obtain a level of proficiency (Shinn, 1989). After determining what rate of growth is necessary, school personnel then identify interventions that enable students to obtain that rate of learning (Lau et al., 2006; Tilly, 2002).

There is a long line of research supporting the effectiveness of functional analysis of problem behaviors to define the problem (Iwata, Dorsey, Slifer, Bauman, & Richman, 1982; Mace, Yankanich, & West, 1988; McComas, Hoch, & Mace, 2000; McComas & Mace, 2000), but few have addressed academic deficits. In 1986, Lentz and Shapiro wrote a seminal paper that laid out the application of functional assessment to academic or learning problems. Their visionary paper raised the idea of systematic assessment of the effect of the environment on student learning and identified variables that might be useful targets for intervention. Shapiro (2004) then presented a particularly useful model in which assessment data were gathered to assess the academic environment, instructional placement, and instructional modifications to define the problem. Moreover, Gickling's model of curriculum-based assessment for instructional design (Gickling & Havertape, 1981) provides a direct approach to design interventions with data (Burns et al., 2004). However, most RtI models use some variation on Howell and Nolet's (2000) curriculum-based evaluation (CBE) that emphasizes task analyses, direct observation, and systematic hypothesis testing. Although research supports the components of this approach, few studies have examined outcomes associated with the model in its entirety.

3. Explore Alternative Solutions to the Problem

Almost all RtI models that currently exist in K–12 schools use a multidisciplinary problem-solving team (PST) to generate alternative solutions for student problems (Burns & Ysseldyke, 2005). Research has consistently supported the use of PSTs to generate potential solutions (Burns & Symington, 2002; Ikeda &

Gustafson, 2002; Marston et al., 2003; Reschly & Starkweather, 1997), but an empirical investigation as to whether such teams are a critical component of RtI has yet to happen. Part of the problem with problem-solving models is that they are vulnerable to inconsistent application across sites. Sites with highly motivated personnel who are well equipped with resources and skills may collect meaningful data and implement interventions effectively. Other sites may not. Because the process does not include specific decision rules and replicable procedures for gathering the data to reach specific decisions, it is vulnerable to misapplication. A key direction for problem-solving models of RtI is to provide great specificity about how problem solutions are generated.

Lentz and Shapiro (1986) provided the framework for testing potential alternative interventions. Following the appearance of this groundbreaking paper, many behavioral researchers began to use single-subject designs to test the effects of certain environmental manipulations on a child's level and rate of learning (Daly, Martens, Dool, & Hintze, 1998; Daly, Martens, Hamler, Dool, Eckert, 1999; Noell et al., 1998). In 1997, Daly, Witt, Martens, and Dool specified a set of common causes of poor academic performance that could be systematically tested with simple assessment procedures. These data and others have led to a well-researched and well-specified set of assessment procedures to identify interventions that will work for an individual student if correctly implemented (Daly et al., 1999; Jones & Wickstrom, 2002). These efforts often are referred to as brief experimental analyses (BEAs) and are becoming commonly researched approaches to identify interventions that are likely to be successful.

Daly and colleagues (Daly et al., 1997, 1998, 1999) proposed the BEA framework for developing reading interventions and have consistently found positive results. A BEA process consists of implementing a series of hypothesis-driven interventions over a short period of time, assessing the immediate effect on the skill in question, and then withdrawing the interventions to return to baseline conditions (Barnett, Daly, Jones, & Lentz, 2004). The BEA assessment technology has been shown to be effective in improving student learning among children with significant reading difficulties (Burns & Wagner, 2008) and to be an effective component of RtI (Barnett et al., 2004; Petursdottir et al., 2009; Wagner, McComas, Bollman, & Holton, 2006).

4. Apply a Solution

Once interventions are found to be effective for an individual student, they are implemented over an extended period, but the delivery system can vary substantially between models. Some models match delivery system with student need and may include special education services as a delivery option (Lau et al.,

2006; Tilly, 2002); others more or less restrict remedial efforts to general education but may utilize individual, small-group, or class-wide interventions (Kovaleski, Tucker, & Stevens, 1996). Generally speaking, interventions implemented to solve a problem are categorized as problem solving or standard protocol, with the defining difference being the uniformity of remedial efforts (Fuchs et al., 2003).

5. Look at the Effects of the Application

Assessment and RtI are almost synonymous terms. Thus, most RtI models consistently examine the effectiveness of interventions as one of their core components (Gresham, 2002). Much of the current RtI research focuses on collecting CBM data (e.g., Christ, 2006; Christ & Ardoin, 2009) and how to best use those data to make decisions (Burns, Scholin, Koscoliek, & Livingston, in press; Burns & Senesac, 2005; Griffiths, VanDerHeyden, Skokut, & Lilles, 2009). In fact, a review of presentations at a recent National Association of School Psychologists Annual Convention found that almost three-fourths of all RtI presentations involved assessment issues (Wackerle, Boice, Christ, & Burns, 2006). The legal provision allowing RtI in K–12 schools has enhanced interest in progress monitoring research, which will continue to inform and improve RtI practice.

Conclusions about Level I Research

The legal provision for RtI created a tension between cognitive and behavioral psychology that has fueled an extensive debate (Burns et al., 2006). The problem-solving model has its roots in behavioral psychology (Gresham, 2007), but certainly other schools of thought influence human learning. Thus, it is difficult to claim that RtI is fundamentally behavioral, but it is consistent with problem solving, which is rooted in behavioral psychology. Moreover, RtI is consistent with prevention science but can be more closely connected by coordinating efforts within schools and coordinating with other community agencies and parents as part of the RtI process.

LEVEL II: DEMONSTRATED EFFECTIVENESS

In addition to consistency with theory, an educational innovation also needs data from applied experimental research of educational outcomes (Ellis, 2005). Research at Level II is conducted in actual schools or in settings similar to those found in schools with little implication for theory. A meta-analysis by Burns and colleagues (2005) found that RtI had large effects on systemic (e.g., reductions in special education referrals) and student (e.g., increase reading scores) outcomes (weighted $d = 1.54$ and 1.02, respectively). Eight studies examined RtI models designed by university faculty and implemented for research purposes, and 16 presented data from existing RtI models in the field, resulting in a weighted d of .92 and 1.42, respectively. Cohen (1988) classified an effect size of .80 or larger as representing a strong effect. Hence, the effect size data reported by Burns et al. (2005) indicated an effective practice.

DON'T FORGET

Tier 2 is the component of an RtI model that may advance student learning outcomes the most by providing an avenue to deliver interventions of known effect to large segments of the school population.

Although the meta-analytic research data just presented are encouraging, additional research regarding specific RtI components is needed and ongoing. Arguably, Tier 2 is the component of an RtI model that may advance student learning outcomes most by providing an avenue to deliver interventions of known effect to large segments of the school population. Tier 1 is the most important tier, and without effective instruction, a solid Tier 2 or 3 will not be useful. However, Tier 2 can address the needs of a large number of students and, if done well, can remediate the deficits of students before Tier 3 is even considered. Moreover, many school districts overload their Tier 3 by moving right to Tier 3 from Tier 1. For example, a school will implement RtI by focusing on quality curriculum and then will utilize a PST approach for all students who struggle. On average, 20% of the student population requires remediation beyond a quality core curriculum (Burns et al., 2005), which suggests that these schools will conduct an in depth-problem analysis while invoking the PST. It is highly likely that the school does not have the resources necessary to implement a successful PST for 20% of the student population. Although we are describing a hypothetical situation, it is one that we see on a regular basis. The school then abandons the PST process as ineffective, but it never had a chance to be successful. Thus, a successful Tier 2 can address the needs of most of the struggling students, leaving only about 2% to 5% (Burns et al., 2005; VanDer-Heyden et al., 2007) of students who need a Tier 3 intervention. Most schools have a chance of successfully implementing a PST and a problem-analysis process with 1% to 5% of the student population.

≡ *Rapid Reference 5.2*

....

Many school districts overload Tier 3 by moving right to Tier 3 from Tier 1. Tier 2 is the key to an effective RtI model.

Because Tier 2 is so important, research is needed that examines the effectiveness of Tier 2 intervention. Vaughn and colleagues (Vaughn et al., in press; Vaughn, Wanzek, Linan-Thompson, & Murray, 2007) provided a structured multicomponent program delivered in daily small-group lessons to students in elementary and middle schools. The results were increased reading skills as compared to control groups, and students who received a Tier 2 intervention scored within the average range on reading measures conducted during the next school year (Vaughn et al, 2007). Similarly, O'Connor, Fulmer, Harty, and Bell (2005) used small-group remediation three times each week for 10 to 15 minutes for kindergarten students and 20 to 25 minutes for students in first, second, or third grades and again found moderate to large differences in post-intervention reading skills as compared to a control group. These data suggest that small-group Tier 2 interventions can be effective; in fact, comparisons between small-group and one-on-one interventions either did not find differential effects (Elbaum, Vaughn, Hughes, & Moody, 2000) or found stronger effects for the small-group interventions (VanDerHeyden, Snyder, Broussard, & Ramsdell, 2008).

The hallmark of Tier 3 interventions has more to do with the intensity of the intervention rather than how they are delivered. Many might assume that Tier 3 interventions are delivered one on one, but, as noted, that may not be necessary. Instead, what is necessary is that the intervention be specific to individual student needs and involve sufficient resources to address those needs. Meta-analytic research has found several effective interventions for students with learning disabilities including mnemonic strategies, various interventions for reading comprehension (e.g., cognitive, cognitive-behavioral, vocabulary, pre- and mid-reading, and direct instruction), behavior modification, and direct instruction (Kavale & Forness, 2000). Moreover, meta-analytic research by Swanson (Swanson, 1999; 2000; Swanson, Hoskyn, & Lee, 1999) identified several components of effective interventions for students with learning disabilities. Given that interventions within Tier 3 are for students with the most severe needs, it seems that the positive effects found in these studies could have positive implications for all Tier 3 interventions, but additional research is needed.

An additional component of Tier 3 is the use of PSTs to develop interventions (Burns & Ysseldyke, 2005). Meta-analytic research found large effects for PSTs, but the effect sizes from PSTs started by university faculty to conduct research were more than twice as large as those that already existed in the field ($d = 1.32$ and .54 respectively; Burns & Symington, 2002). Thus, research regarding PSTs suggests that they are an effective practice, but the relatively low effects of studies involving PSTs that existed in the field suggests that implementation integrity may have been low (Kovaleski, Gickling, Morrow, & Swank, 1998).

Conclusions about Level II Research

In addition to being consistent with theory, there are data to support the effectiveness of interventions and processes (e.g., PST) used within RtI. Moreover, meta-analytic research found large effects for RtI models in their entirety. However, the breadth and scope of the RtI research was fairly limited. Additional rigorous research is needed that examines the effects of implementing an RtI model. Moreover, Shapiro and Clemens (2009) provide a framework with which RtI models can be evaluated. Practitioners are encouraged to use that framework to evaluate their model, and researchers should use the framework to study RtI models that exist within the field to publish the outcome data in national journals.

LEVEL III: CONSISTENT IMPLEMENTATION

The third level of research for educational innovations suggested by Ellis (2005) addresses implementation because even interventions based on sound theory with proven effectiveness will not lead to improved outcomes if they are not implemented correctly. The goal of Level III research is to determine the effects of program implementation at the school or district level.

Several scholars have identified implementation integrity as a potential fatal flaw in RtI (Burns, 2007; Gansle & Noell, 2007; Noell & Gansle, 2006; Ysseldyke, 2005). Implementation integrity is especially important given the direct relationship between correct implementation of an RtI model and student outcomes (Kovaleski et al., 1998; Telzrow, McNamara, & Hollinger, 2000). Several studies have examined the effect of performance feedback on the integrity with which interventions are implemented (Codding, Feinburg, Dunn, & Pace, 2005; Mortenson & Witt, 1998; Noell, Duhon, Gatti, & Connell, 2002; Noell, Witt, Gilbertson, Ranier, & Freeland, 1997; Noell et al., 2000, 2005; Witt, Noell, LaFleur, & Mortenson, 1997); one of these studies examined implementation within the context of RtI (Duhon, Mesmer, Gregerson, & Witt, 2009).

DON'T FORGET
....
Tiered interventions have existed within public health models for decades, and schools across the country were using RtI data to enhance learning and to make SLD identification decisions 20 years ago.

Although correct implementation of the intervention is an important aspect of RtI, there are many other components for which implementation integrity are important including the PST process, use of decision rules, team meetings, data collection, and implementing the core curriculum. Performance feedback has been used to successfully enhance the integrity with which the PST process is implemented (Burns, Peters, & Noell, 2008), but research regarding the other areas is quite limited or nonexistent, and suggests areas of potential decision-making error (see Chapter 3).

Performance feedback can enhance implementation integrity and could be applied to various RtI components in research and practice. Moreover, in vivo training could also enhance integrity because those who are asked to implement the intervention may not actually know how to do so (Gansle & Noell, 2007). Training, and its impact on RtI implementation, appears to be an area in need of considerable research. We currently do not know how well preservice school personnel are trained in the principles of RtI, but our experience suggests that most begin their professional experience with limited understanding of and skills necessary for RtI implementation. Moreover, we do not know if in vivo training could enhance RtI implementation and if pairing it with other interventions (e.g., performance feedback, incentives) would enhance its potential positive effect.

In addition to a lack of research about how to enhance implementation integrity within RtI, there is a considerable need for research about implementation of various components of RtI. Reschly, Coolong-Chaffin, Christenson, and Gutkin (2007) point out the importance of considering the classroom ecology and parental engagement in education, but these topics are almost completely absent from the RtI literature.

Conclusions about Level III Research

Unfortunately, Level III research is the least likely of the three types of research to be conducted (Ellis, 2005), which seems to be the case with RtI. There are potential causes for optimism given the effects of performance feedback on intervention and PST implementation. However, the research regarding implementation of an RtI model is considerably lacking.

STRENGTHS AND WEAKNESSES

It is difficult to make any summative statements about RtI research given that the research is ongoing. We know a great deal about how to implement RtI, but there is still much more to learn. Next we list the strengths and weaknesses of RtI research and implementation.

Strengths

RtI was clearly derived from a sound theoretical basis and a long line of empirical inquiry. In fact, some have suggested that RtI represents a rare case of practice and policy catching up with science (K. Gibbons, personal communication, 2007). This might be an optimistic interpretation of the state of affairs, but it does adequately capture the solid research base on which RtI functions.

RtI is not a new practice. Tiered interventions have existed within public health models for decades, and schools across the country were using RtI data to enhance learning and to make SLD identification decisions 20 years ago (Graden, Stollar, & Poth, 2007; Lau et al., 2006). Researchers have examined the use of student response to interventions to make decisions (Tucker, 2001; Vellutino et al., 1996), and policy recommendations to use RtI first occurred almost 30 years ago (Heller, Holtzman, & Messick, 1982). There is considerable research from which to draw and lessons learned from over 20 years of practical implementation.

Although the research regarding the effectiveness of RtI models in their entirety is limited, what we have is quite convincing. Moreover, numerous individual studies and meta-analyses of the effectiveness of various interventions and intervention plan components provide cause for optimism. Finally, RtI relevant measurement research has almost literally exploded since RtI became part of the federal law, and we now understand in considerably greater depth how to measure student learning and how to use those data for valid decision making.

We consider it a strength that much of the focus of RtI is on improving student learning rather than SLD identification. Gerber (2005) stated that RtI does not inform us about learning disabilities, but, as stated earlier, measuring how much a student actually learns seems central to a SLD diagnosis. We are not convinced that RtI will enhance our understanding of learning disabilities but agree that it will substantially improve our understanding of individual student learning. Thus, perhaps we should conceptualize a SLD diagnosis within RtI as a means rather than an end, and in doing so we will enhance student learning both for entire schools and for one student at a time.

We have observed numerous data meetings, PSTs, and various teacher collaborative efforts since the implementation of RtI and are encouraged by the conversations we hear. In our opinion, teachers are *finally* asking the right questions. It seems that for decades we assumed that the source of student difficulty lay within the student (e.g., SLD, attention deficit disorder, laziness), and certainly no one would argue the relevance of some student characteristics to learning. However, teachers and other school personnel are now viewing the child as someone who is learning in a particular context and direct their conversations to student-environment fit, are using data in meaningful ways, and are invigorated by the sense of efficacy that they now feel. Clearly we have a long way to go in regard to RtI implementation, but change takes time and begins with addressing the attitudes, beliefs, and behaviors of those who actually implement the change (Sarason, 1996). We are seeing different attitudes, beliefs, and behaviors.

Weaknesses

School personnel can feel confident in their actions if they implement RtI in a manner that is consistent with the model we describe in this book. However, we have more to learn, and practitioners should begin by acknowledging that their RtI implementation efforts may look very different as they implement them. The model may evolve as school personnel better understand their school's unique needs and as subsequent research on RtI implementation continues to inform practice. Listed next are areas of weakness in RtI research and areas where future research will inform future practice.

As emphasized, consistent implementation has to be a top priority among RtI researchers. We have to better understand not only how to ensure that treatment integrity occurs for individual and group interventions but also how the RtI process and various components can be implemented with integrity on a consistent basis. More specifically, the lack of research on parental engagement is troubling because it affects both implementation and the theoretical foundation for RtI. If we accept that RtI developed from and is consistent with prevention science, then coordination of prevention activities is imperative. The most basic coordination should be between the school and the students' homes. Research has examined the effects of home-school partnerships and how to achieve them, but those data have yet to be adequately applied to RtI implementation.

It is largely unknown how school personnel explore possible alternatives to solve problems. Most would likely report the use of CBE, but there is sparse research evaluating the effectiveness of CBE, and it is a somewhat complex process that is not easy to implement. BEAs provide a possible alternative, but how often those are used in schools is unknown. We need a more systematic approach to problem analysis and solving problems.

Although there is considerable research on which RtI is based and convincing data about the effectiveness of RtI, there are limited data about math and writing and even less about implementation in high schools and middle schools. Burns (2008) suggests models for high school implementation, and Windram, Scierka, and Silberglitt (2007) describe a specific high school implementation model and present convincing outcome data. However, information about secondary settings is limited.

Given that implementation integrity is a significant concern, we need to know a great deal more about preservice and inservice professional development. Fortunately, many colleges of education and school psychology programs graduate personnel with the necessary skills (e.g., CBM, data-based decision making, interventions, consultation, problem solving), but rarely are those skills directly contextualized within RtI. Moreover, we need effective inservice professional development models to support the implementation among the thousands of teachers and other school personnel already working in the field. In our opinion, incorporating RtI within pre- and inservice curricula is perhaps the single most important moderator to successful RtI implementation, but it may also be the least likely to occur.

CAUTION

Valid decision making within RtI is not an easy process. There are more opportunities for error than in static assessment models of achievement-ability discrepancies, which also were poorly implemented. School personnel will have to establish and strictly adhere to decision rules and collect interobserver agreement data to ensure validity of the process.

Valid decision making within RtI is not an easy process. There are more opportunities for error than in static assessment models of achievement-ability discrepancies, which also were poorly implemented (Scruggs & Mastropieri, 2002). School personnel will have to establish and strictly adhere to decision rules and collect interobserver agreement data to ensure validity of the process. Of course, the assessment process is important, but we cannot focus on assessment to the neglect of intervention. We cannot move in a direction away from "wait to fail" toward "watch them fail" (Reynolds & Shawyitz, 2009a, p. 130).

Decades of school effectiveness research found that the only variable that always mattered was effective *instructional* leadership by the school principal (Levine & Lezotte, 1990). However, leadership models within RtI are not well articulated. The National Association of State Directors of Special Education has sponsored blueprints for RtI implementation at the school building (Kurns & Tilly, 2008) and district level (Elliott & Morrison, 2008), but those brief yet helpful documents do not fully discuss leadership issues such as personnel development, human resources, and allocating noninstructional resources. Thus, more work and models to follow are needed in this area.

SUMMARY

Educational innovations come and go with alarming frequency, and RtI has the potential to join the long list of "abandoned shipwrecks" (Ellis, 2005, p. 200) despite consistency with theory, a solid research base, and consistently demonstrated effectiveness. As is usually the case, research is the key. If we can develop sound implementation protocols and find methods to ensure that they are followed, if we can actively engage parents and community agencies in the process, and if we can continue to evolve our practices based on cutting-edge research, then RtI will fulfill its potential effects for students and systems.

🐾 TEST-YOURSELF QUESTIONS 🐾

1. **What are the essential characteristics of a prevention science?**
2. **What are some of the causal factors for low achievement that are addressed by RtI and contribute to prevention of SLD?**
3. **Triaging students into varying intensity levels of intervention based on a single universal screening data point is an empirically supported practice.**
   True or False?
4. **Identify the most significant threat to RtI decision making.**
5. **Brief experimental analysis can be used to identify intervention facets that have a positive effect on student learning.**
   True or False?
6. **What is the most effective way to ensure implementation integrity in RtI?**

Answers
1. Address causal factors for the problem, address risk factors before they stabilize, target individuals who are at high risk for intervention, and coordinate actions in each domain of functioning.

(continued)

2. RtI enhances core instruction and targets learning deficits through increasingly intense interventions, thus repairing existing learning deficits and preventing the need for SLD diagnosis.
3. False. Universal screening data alone are not an adequate basis for determining intervention intensity. Follow-up assessment is required.
4. Correct implementation of RtI procedures and data interpretation.
5. True.
6. Use of performance feedback.

Six

CLINICAL APPLICATIONS OF RTI

COMMON CHALLENGES RTI CAN BE USED TO ADDRESS

Response to intervention (RtI) can be transformational for systems. Because RtI efforts are guided by effects on student learning, many systemic improvements are possible, and RtI can become a vehicle for system improvement. Universal screening and targeted intervention rule out potential threats to the accuracy of the initial risk decision including biased referral sources (Bahr & Fuchs, 1991) and decision errors arising from high-prevalence situations (e.g., many students are low achieving in a particular setting; VanDerHeyden & Witt, 2005).

Disproportionate Identification by Ethnicity, Gender, and Poverty Status

Algozzine, Ysseldyke, and Christenson (1983) conducted a large-scale survey study examining referral and placement rates and reported that 92% of referred students were tested and 73% of those students qualified and were placed in special programs. During the next decade, most school districts implemented programs designed to reduce the number of students receiving a formal eligibility evaluation (e.g., prereferral problem-solving committees, mandated prereferral interventions). Despite the implementation of these programs, Ysseldyke, Vanderwood, and Shriner (1997) replicated Algozzine et al.'s study and obtained remarkably similar results. Again, 72% of referred students were placed in some form of special education, and most were placed in the category for which they were referred.

The degree to which teachers accurately identify students at risk has been a topic of much debate. Many researchers have found that teachers' ratings of student capability and direct measures of student capability generally correspond, but with two notable findings. First, teacher ratings tend to reflect potential inequities related to ethnicity and gender. In a direct comparison of teacher-based referral and curriculum-based measurement (CBM) referral, females in the teacher-referred group tended to exhibit problem behaviors more frequently than did females in a CBM-referred group (Marston, Mirkin, & Deno, 1984). Moreover, teachers tended to refer the lowest-achieving students for special services but referred more African American students and more male students than would be expected according to base rate occurrence of low-achieving African American students and low-achieving males in the sample (Shinn, Tindall, & Spira, 1987). Marston et al. (1984) found that the performance of teacher-referred students did not significantly differ from CBM-referred students, but males and females were more equally represented when referral was based on CBM scores.

> **CAUTION**
>
> Universal screening alone is insufficient to repair inequities in identification. Rather, it is the intervention component that improves referral accuracy and equity.

Gresham, MacMillan, and Bocian (1997) found that teachers could discriminate students in need of special services from so-called normals but could not distinguish between students who were low achieving, diagnosed with a learning disability, and diagnosed with mild mental retardation. Researchers have also found that the overreferral of minority students may be associated with legitimate risk (i.e., lower achievement for referred students; Bahr & Fuchs, 1991; Hosp & Reschly, 2004). VanDerHeyden and Witt (2005) examined the accuracy of teacher referral relative to a number of other potential identification sources and found that teacher referral was highly unstable across high-achieving and low-achieving classrooms and that RtI as an identification source enhanced referral accuracy (yielding the strongest sensitivity and specificity estimates) that was proportionate by race and sex. Importantly, their findings indicated that universal screening alone is insufficient to repair inequities in identification. Rather, it is the intervention component that improves referral accuracy and equity.

Overidentification

With identification rates soaring in many districts, school systems are rightfully concerned about the degree to which students' needs are being met in the most effective and efficient way possible. Because superior outcomes have not been associated with placement in special education for students with a specific learning disability (SLD) relative to similarly at-risk peers (Kavale & Forness, 1999), many decision makers question the value of SLD-driven service delivery, especially in light of evidence of strong effects for direct intervention in foundation skills particularly in the area of early reading (O'Connor, White, & Swanson, 2007; Torgesen et al., 1999; Torgesen, 2001; Vellutino et al., 1996). Research on RtI implementations has demonstrated improved reading performance outcomes for students exposed to intervention through RtI-like systems in research studies (Torgesen et al., 1999; Vaughn et al., 2003). Marked reductions in the numbers of students evaluated and placed into special education have been reported in district-wide trials (Bollman, Silberglitt, & Gibbons, 2007; Sornson, Frost, & Burns, 2005) along with improved diagnostic accuracy as indicated by higher percentages of those students who were evaluated as qualifying for services (VanDerHeyden, Witt, & Gilbertson, 2007).

DON'T FORGET

Effective interventions include frequent progress monitoring using direct, brief measures of student performance like CBM along with fluency-building interventions that emphasize modeling, guided practice, and error correction.

Low Achievement

Research findings indicate that RtI can be used to accelerate student learning. Specifically, a number of research studies demonstrate high success rates for those students exposed to intervention (VanDerHeyden & Burns, 2005) even when the students exposed to intervention include those who are most at risk or lowest achieving (O'Connor, White, & Swanson, 2007; Torgeson et al., 1999; Vaughn, Linan-Thompon, & Hickman, 2003). Interventions reported in the literature have included well-validated strategies, such as frequent progress monitoring using direct, brief measures of student performance like CBM along with fluency-building interventions that emphasize modeling, guided practice, and error correction.

Identifying Areas of Needed Intervention at the System and Student Level

To attain positive effects on student and system outcomes, screening data must be examined to identify potential intervention targets. As long as a screening task has been correctly selected and administered, universal screening data can be used to indicate where large numbers of students experience difficulty and to assist in pinpointing any potential common variables shared among those students that might explain the poor performance (and thus be a rich target for systemic intervention). Examples of system problems include grade-wide or class-wide problems. Common potential causes of grade-wide and class-wide problems include inadvertent or deliberate tracking of students, students who have not mastered prerequisite skills, ongoing instructional problems in the instructional environment (e.g., calendar of instruction, pacing of instruction, adequacy of instruction). A recent comprehensive research synthesis examining potential Tier 1 intervention programs in mathematics (Slavin & Lake, 2008) found only modest effect sizes for published curricula (about .10), better but still modest effect sizes for computer-based computational fluency interventions offered as a supplement to core instruction (about .19), and moderate (.40) effect sizes for interventions that changed the instructional interaction in the classroom (i.e., increased students' opportunities to respond with corrective feedback on instructional-level materials). Hence, where many students seem to be struggling, the instructional basics can be checked. Efforts to repair instructional problems pay large dividends in improving the targeted skill but also in preventing more widespread learning deficits over time and across content areas. Tables 2.2 and 2.3 in Chapter 2 offer specific recommendations for evaluating screening data to detect system problems and develop systemic interventions.

DON'T FORGET

Common potential causes of grade-wide and class-wide problems include inadvertent or deliberate tracking of students, students who have not mastered prerequisite skills, and ongoing instructional problems in the instructional environment (e.g., calendar of instruction, pacing of instruction, adequacy of instruction).

IDENTIFICATION OF SPECIFIC LEARNING DISABILITIES USING RTI

Perhaps the RtI application about which practitioners are most concerned is the use of the data to make SLD identification decisions. The Individuals with Disabilities Education Act of 2004 (IDEA) states that when making SLD identification decisions, local educational agencies "shall not be required to take into consideration whether a child has a severe discrepancy between achievement and intellectual ability" and "may use a process that determines if the child responds to scientific, research-based intervention as a part of the evaluation procedures" (Public Law No. 108–446 § 614 [b][6][A]; § 614 [b][2 & 3]). Although most RtI advocates emphasize its potential role in enhancing student learning, the foundation for its existence comes from special education eligibility decisions.

Before we discuss *how* to make eligibility decisions, we will discuss *when* to make them. The federal IDEA regulations require that school personnel convene an Evaluation Review in which the specific assessment plan is outlined, including which tests will be administered and for what purposes, and parents provide informed consent for the evaluation. As Gansle and Noell (2005) point out, using RtI data for eligibility decisions without ensuring that RtI actually occurs is much like convening an Evaluation Review, holding an Individualized Educational Program Team meeting within 60 calendar days, and diagnosing a student as SLD without ever administering any of the tests that were listed at the Evaluation Review. Thus, in order to use the data for eligibility decisions, school personnel should have data to support that (a) their plan included a research-based model for RtI, (b) the model was implemented as designed, and (c) the interventions actually occurred. The process of providing a legally defensible RtI model centers on documenting the implementation integrity of the decision-making rules, the problem-solving (and problem-solving team) process, and interventions. Table 3.1 in Chapter 3 of this book summarizes the basic components that RtI models share and upon which decision validity hinges. The table includes a summary of signs that error has occurred compromising the validity of the RtI decision.

CAUTION

To use the data for eligibility decisions, school personnel should have data to support that (a) their plan included a research-based model for RtI, (b) the model was implemented as designed, and (c) the interventions actually occurred. Table 3.1 includes a summary of signs that RtI implementation error has occurred that compromises the validity of the RtI decision.

Special Education and RtI

Special education is defined as individualized instruction to meet the unique needs of a child with a disability (Public Law No. 108–446). Tier 3 is the most intensive tier of intervention and is highly individualized. Thus, Tier 3 and special education serve a similar role: individualized instruction to meet unique needs. As such, it is quite possible and perhaps preferable for special education to be a service provided within Tier 3. Special education teachers can be involved in

Tiers 2 and 3, including direct service, but as a general education service because IDEA now allows for up to 15% of special education funding to be used for early intervention. Thus, it is possible for a special education teacher to conduct a small-group intervention, deliver one-on-one intervention, consult with grade-level teams, participate in screening activities, and so on, all under the auspices of general education.

Identification of SLD in many RtI models is conducted post-intervention. RtI should involve a seamless continuum of services in which students fluidly transition between intervention groups and tiers of intervention; and the seamless continuum should include special education. However, the seamless continuum is not possible until RtI data are used for eligibility purposes, which is possible only after the school's RtI model is fully implemented. Until then, Tiers 2 and 3 should be considered essentially prereferral services in which special education occurs after Tier 3 interventions. After full implementation, special education becomes a seamless service provided within Tier 3.

RtI Outcomes and SLD

Progress-monitoring data are used to make decisions within an RtI model, including SLD identification. These data are used to judge one of four possible outcomes (Riley-Tillman & Burns, 2009). First, the intervention will be successful and the student(s) will make sufficient progress and demonstrate proficient skills. This is the most desirable and, it is hoped, frequent outcome that would result in stopping the intervention. Second, the intervention will be effective and the student will make sufficient progress but still will score in the at-risk range. In this scenario, the intervention would likely continue, but the intervention tier would remain.

The third and fourth possibilities could involve SLD identification. As described in Chapter 4, a student's progress monitoring data might result in a slope of growth that falls below a normative standard (e.g., 1 standard deviation below the mean) and the score remains within an at-risk range (as determined by Dynamic Indicators of Early Literacy Skills [DIBELS] standards or scoring below the 25th percentile on a national norm), which is the definition of a dual discrepancy (DD). When a dual discrepancy is apparent, the intervention is judged as not effective, and a more intense intervention is implemented. A student receiving a Tier 2 intervention would likely be given a Tier 3 intervention. A student receiving a Tier 3 intervention that results in a dual discrepancy could be considered for SLD identification. When this happens, it is critically important to determine that the student actually did not respond to the evidence-based intervention by establishing that intervention was implemented with fidelity and that the progress-monitoring data were psychometrically sound and appropriately collected.

The fourth possible outcome is that the student makes sufficient progress but still is considerably below proficiency, and the intervention is so intense that it cannot be reasonably continued within the parameters of general education. In a "true" RtI model, this is the acceptable pathway to SLD. RtI is not a search to find students who are "truly SLD" but a search to find what will help students learn. As stated, special education is a resource that can be applied to the most severe learning difficulties, but only if the intervention will facilitate student learning.

Special Education Procedures

Although special education is conceptualized somewhat differently in an RtI model than in a more traditional approach to service delivery, the same rules and regulations apply. In other words, procedures such as Evaluation Reviews, informed consent, and the like are still in place and student's needs still are written into an Individualized Educational Program (IEP), as mandated by law. However, the process is often much quicker than in traditional systems.

A referral for an SLD evaluation is made when a grade-level team suspects a disability, which in an RtI model involves a dual discrepancy after a research-based intervention is implemented with integrity or an acceptable rate of growth is attained due to an intervention that is too intensive to sustain in general education. When one of these situations occurs, the grade-level team makes a referral to a multidisciplinary evaluation team who then conducts an Evaluation Review with the students' parents in order to obtain informed consent. At that time the multidisciplinary evaluation team will examine the progress-monitoring and other existing data to determine if any additional data are needed. It is likely that no additional data are needed or perhaps minimal data, such as a standardized test of achievement. Thus, the referral and evaluation process still would require only the 60 calendar days or less because it involves examining data that already exist. It is a common misconception that RtI will delay referrals to special education because students have to receive a Tier 2 and 3 intervention before they can be referred. However, eligibility decisions within an RtI model are not made by putting a student through a three-tiered intervention model after suspecting a disability; they are made by examining the data that already exist from a multitiered intervention system that is already in place.

As is currently true, a referral for special education eligibility can be made at any time, and the school is legally obligated to oblige. However, the school can examine RtI data and determine that eligibility is not warranted or that RtI data are sufficient to make an SLD diagnosis. Collecting data to determine appropriate instructional strategies (e.g., Tier 2 or Tier 3) does not require parental consent (Alexander, 2006). Moreover, the *Johnson v. Upland* (2002) decision ruled that schools can use less intense interventions prior to evaluation for special education, which suggests that the RtI process will not be litigiously interpreted as an unreasonable delay in the determination of special education eligibility as long as academic progress is documented and a referral for evaluation is made as soon as a disability is suspected (Burns, Wagner, & Jacob, 2008). Although consent is not required for interventions, parents should be notified if any ongoing involvement is anticipated (National Association of School Psychologists, 2000).

Comprehensive Evaluation

The multidisciplinary evaluation team could examine the RtI data and conclude that no additional data are needed to make an SLD diagnosis. They could also decide that specific data are needed to answer a specific question or to inform the components of the students IEP, such as: (a) student's current levels of academic achievement and functional performance; (b) measurable annual goals; (c) measuring progress toward meeting the annual goals; or (d) deciding what special education and related services and supplementary aids and services are needed (Public Law No. 108–466 § 614 [d][1][A]). However, RtI data seem especially well suited to address these four components (Burns et al., 2008).

RtI data are helpful when writing an IEP, but the RtI provision does not eliminate the requirement for a comprehensive evaluation. The requirement for an individual and comprehensive evaluation remained mostly unchanged in the past three versions of IDEA, including the most recent one (Public Law No. 108–466 § 614 [a][1][A]) that allowed the use of RtI as part of the process. Federal regulations require that a variety of assessment tools be used to gather relevant functional and developmental information about the child, and the child be assessed in all areas related to the suspected disability including, if appropriate, health, vision, hearing, social and emotional status, general intelligence, academic performance, communicative status, and motor abilities (34 C.F.R. 300.532). The key concept in these requirements is that the data should be functionally related to the specific problem. There is no reason to assess, for example, motor abilities as part of a standard assessment package, and certainly very few people would argue for vision and hearing screenings as part of all SLD evaluations. Thus, assessments of general intelligence have no more or no less of a legal justification than vision screenings, especially given the well-documented irrelevance of IQ in intervention design or student outcomes (Siegel, 1988; Stuebing et al., 2002; Vellutino, Scanlon, & Lyon, 2000). Moreover, the U.S. Department of Education's Office of Special Education Programs (2009) stated that measures of cognitive processing and general aptitude should not be part of an SLD evaluation because there is "no current evidence that such assessments are necessary or sufficient for identifying SLD" (p. 46651). However, advocates for RtI support that measures of aptitude and cognitive processing should be administered when appropriate, but acknowledge that they would rarely inform the intervention or identification process (Gresham et al., 2005).

SUMMARY

The RtI provision has already changed the face of assessment within special education. The requirement for a comprehensive evaluation in an RtI framework will likely be met by assessing a variety of constructs including teachable skills, prior and current instructional opportunities, and instructional variables such as time allocated for instruction, pace of instruction, number of opportunities to respond, and sequencing of skills rather than constructs for which the relationship to learning is less direct (Gresham et al., 2005). Moreover, using RtI data for SLD identification results in data that are highly likely to be multifaceted, fair, valid, and useful (Burns et al., 2008). There certainly is more research to be conducted and several potential threats to validity within the process, but schools that are implementing multitiered systems of intervention with fidelity and using the data for important decision making are acting in an ethical and legally defensible manner.

🐟 TEST-YOURSELF QUESTIONS 🐟

1. **What common system challenges can be addressed via RtI?**
2. **RtI data can be used to diagnose SLD without direct evidence of use of a research-based RtI model with evidence of intervention implementation.** True or False?
3. **When does referral for evaluation occur in RtI?**
   (a) Following poor response to a Tier 3 intervention implemented with integrity for a sufficient period of time.
   (b) Following an acceptable response to an intervention that is too intensive to sustain in the general education environment.

(continued)

(c) Following teacher referral.

(d) a or b.

(e) None of the above.

4. **When an adult indicates suspicion of disability, RtI is initiated, and a referral occurs only after a child has had a failed response to intervention at Tiers 2 and 3.**

   True or False?

5. **RtI delays diagnosis of SLD.**

   True or False?

Answers

1. Disproportionate identification by ethnicity, gender, and poverty status; overidentification; and low achievement.
2. False.
3. d
4. False. RtI is an ongoing process where screening data are routinely evaluated to identify students in need of intervention, intervention is delivered, and intervention effects are evaluated.
5. False. RtI should not delay diagnosis. Rather, RtI efforts should be examined to ensure that services are being provided to students rapidly and that students are demonstrating growth or the intervention is being iteratively adjusted. Implementation errors should be dealt with directly and rapidly so that delays do not occur.

Seven

CASE REPORT ILLUSTRATIONS

CASE EXAMPLE: SUCCESSFUL CLASS-WIDE INTERVENTION FOR MATHEMATICS

During universal screening in mathematics in fourth grade, a class-wide learning problem was detected (class median score below criterion on a grade-level-appropriate skill). Examination of mean and median scores for all fourth-grade teachers at the school revealed that this fourth-grade class was the lowest-performing fourth-grade class in the school and the only class with a class-wide problem.

Figure 7.1 shows the mean and median score for each of the fourth-grade teachers during universal screening on the mathematics measure. Classroom 6 is the lowest-performing room and below criterion. Other classes are performing above criterion, which rules out a grade-wide learning problem in mathematics.

Figure 7.2 shows each student's performance in the class relative to the screening criterion. In this class, the majority of students performed below criterion on a grade-level task that is a prerequisite skill for successful mathematics learning at fourth grade.

To evaluate the adequacy of the screening decision, implementers must verify that an appropriate skill was selected for screening and that the screening procedures were correctly followed. (See Appendix A.) In this case, the skill assessed during the fall screening was multiplication facts 0–12. This skill was determined to be appropriate, given local expectations for learning in mathematics (i.e., the fourth-grade program of instruction emphasized multi-digit multiplication and division work and progressed in the spring to working with proportions via decimals, percentages, and fractions). Administration integrity data were available indicating that the screening assessment had been correctly administered. Because a class-wide learning problem was detected, the next step

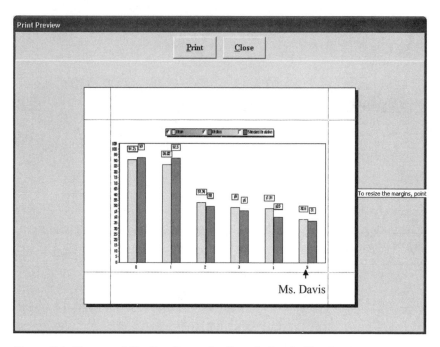

Figure 7.1 Mean and Median Score for Fourth-Grade Teachers.

Source: Graph created on iSTEEP software, www.isteep.com.

(see Figure 7.3) involved identifying patterns in the universal screening data that would serve as high-yield intervention and prevention targets. An observation in the classroom indicated that instructional basics were adequate. (See Appendix C.) Every item had a "yes" checked indicating that instructional basics in the classroom were intact. Analyzing the screening data indicated that students were missing prerequisite skills.

Class-wide intervention was planned and initiated in Ms. Davis's class. The intervention was intended to supplement Tier 1 instruction and build fluency on a number of skills considered prerequisite to successful math instruction at fourth grade. Class-wide intervention began with multiplication facts 0–12 (Figure 7.4). When the median score reached the mastery criterion for that skill, the intervention progressed to division facts 0–12 (Figure 7.5). When the median score reached mastery on that skill, intervention progressed to fact families for multiplication and division 0–12 (Figure 7.6), and then adding and subtracting decimals (Figure 7.7).

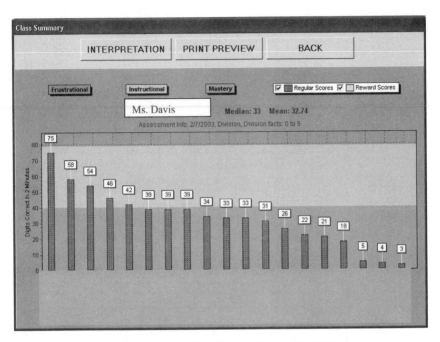

Figure 7.2 Student Performance Relative to Screening Criterion.

Source: Graph created on iSTEEP software, www.isteep.com.

All students performed in the instructional range or higher given instruction, so no students were identified for Tier 3 intervention. At this point during intervention it was time for the winter screening. The winter screening assessed more skills and was more challenging than the fall screening task. A class-wide problem was no longer detected in Ms. Davis's classroom (see Figure 7.8).

CASE EXAMPLE: TIER 3 SUCCESSFUL AND UNSUCCESSFUL INTERVENTION

Figure 7.9 shows the median score for a class during each week of Tier 2 intervention designed to supplement and enhance instruction occurring at Tier 1 in a second-grade classroom.

This class also shows a positive and successful response to intervention. As intervention persists, two students, Josh and Kim, begin to lag noticeably behind their classmates. Because the class median has reached mastery and Josh's and Kim's performance remains in the frustration range, Josh and Kim should receive Tier 3 intervention for mathematics. (See Figure 7.10.)

Step 1	Rule out class-wide problem. → (Print class-wide and grade-wide graphs with criterion reference.)	Proceed to individual assessment and intervention as needed.		Ms. Davis's class
Step 2	If class-wide problem is not ruled out, consider... →	Was measurement task appropriate?		*Yes*
		Was measurement correctly administered?		*Yes*
		Common features of classes apparent? →	By grade?	*No*
			By content?	*Yes, math only*
			By particular teachers?	*Yes, Ms. Davis's class at 4th grade*
			Are students being tracked?	*No*
			Demographic features of students?	*Proportionate*
		Look backward. →	Prerequisite skills mastered?	*No*
			Rapid increase in content difficulty or expectations for learning?	*Yes*
		Look forward. →	Deficits apparent at subsequent grade levels?	*Yes, 2/4 class-wide problems at 6th grade*

Figure 7.3 Analysis of Screening Data for Intervention and Prevention Planning.

Step 3	PRIORITIZE intervention targets.	Consider patterns and prioritize (by grade, by content, by demographics, others).	Mathematics
Step 4	COORDINATE efforts to . . .	Repair existing problems.	*Class-wide intervention Ms. Davis: Three classes just above criterion.*
		Prevent future problems.	*Increase difficulty of end-of-year screening at 3rd grade; monitor 4th-grade progress monthly to ensure mastery of key learning objectives.*
Step 5	EVALUATE solutions.	Monitor % of class-wide problems.	*at 4th-grade fall, winter, and spring screening*
		% of grade-wide problems.	*at 3rd, 4th, and 5th fall, winter, spring*
		% of students below criterion on screening (by demographic features).	*at fall, winter, and spring screening*

Figure 7.3 (continued)

119

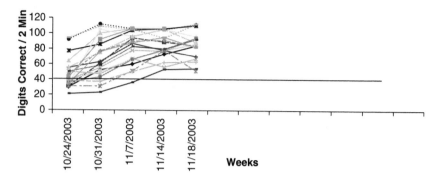

Figure 7.4 Ms. Davis Multiplication 0–12.

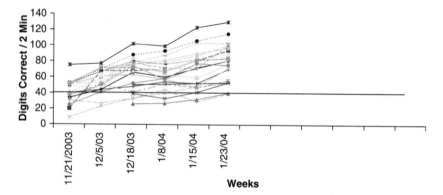

Figure 7.5 Ms. Davis Division 0–12.

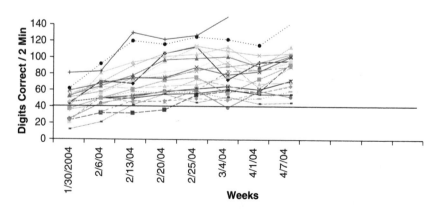

Figure 7.6 Ms. Davis Fact Family Multiplication/Division 0–12.

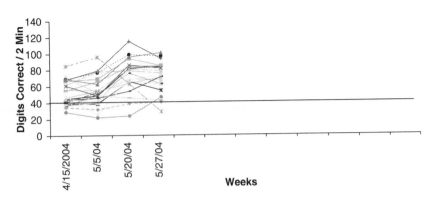

Figure 7.7 Ms. Davis Add and Subtract Decimals.

To plan the Tier 3 intervention, Josh participated in a brief assessment session conducted outside of the classroom with the school psychologist. Total assessment time required less than 20 minutes. Josh was given a fact families worksheet for addition and subtraction facts 0–20. Josh's class had made rapid progress on

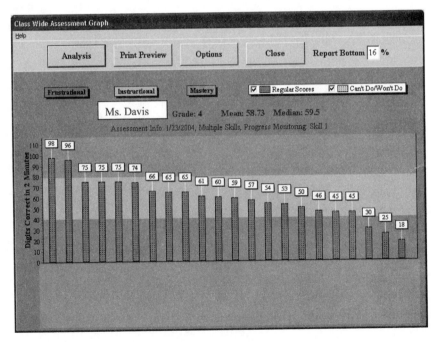

Figure 7.8 Class-Wide Assessment Graph.

Source: Graph created on iSTEEP software, www.isteep.com.

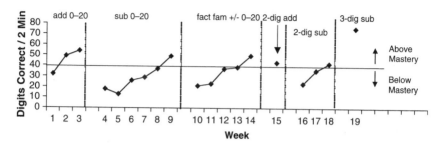

Figure 7.9 Second-Grade Teacher Intervention Progress.

this skill; the median score reached the mastery criterion with only three weeks of supplemental intervention. Josh scored in the frustration range for that skill, and offering tangible incentives did not improve his performance. Further assessment (sampling back through lower-level skills) indicated that Josh was not fluent in basic subtraction facts. When given a subtraction 0–20 probe, he scored 15 digits correct per 2 minutes, which is in the frustration range. With brief instruction, which included modeling correct problem completion, guided practice solving subtraction problems, and a timed interval of independent practice, Josh's score improved to 20 digits correct per minute. Hence, individual intervention was conducted using that protocol for Josh for subtraction 0–20 (See Figure 7.11). The classroom teacher administered intervention daily. She was

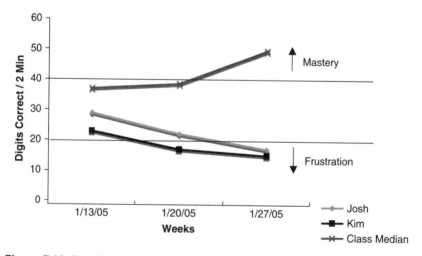

Figure 7.10 Fact Families Add/Subtract 0–20.

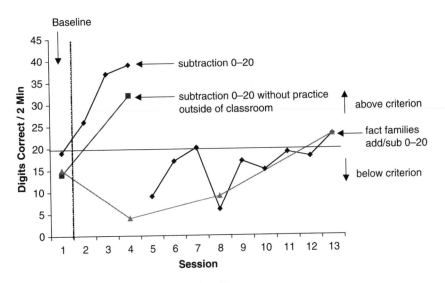

Figure 7.11 Josh's Math Intervention Progress.

provided with all necessary materials to conduct the intervention and was observed to complete all the steps independently and correctly in a training session before conducting the intervention on her own. After 4 days of intervention, the school psychologist reviewed the intervention progress and conducted a generalization check by administering the criterion-level assessment probe for fact families for addition and subtraction 0–20. Performance on the criterion-level probe (fact families) did not reach the intervention success criterion, so intervention continued for another week. Because Josh reached the mastery criterion for subtraction 0–20, the difficulty of the materials was advanced so that intervention occurred for fact families for the following week. A graph of Josh's performance was shared with the teacher, and she was provided all the necessary materials to continue for another week. Following another week of intervention, Josh again was pulled briefly out of the classroom by the school psychologist to complete a generalization check. Because performance during the second week of intervention was variable, an integrity check was conducted in the classroom. The time of day that the intervention was being conducted was altered to a time that the teacher felt would work better for Josh. The teacher was provided with materials to continue another week. At the end of the third week, Josh scored 23 digits correct per 2 minutes on the fact families probe of addition and subtraction 0–20 without practice and outside of the classroom setting. Because this score met the RtI success criterion, Josh was determined to have had a successful response to individual intervention. A brief meeting was held with the classroom teacher and Josh's parents to discuss how to support higher-quality performance from Josh in the area of mathematics in the classroom. Josh's parents were particularly pleased to know that routine screening would detect if Josh fell behind his classmates again in the future.

Kim also was identified to receive Tier 3 intervention. Following the completion of intervention for Josh, the classroom teacher agreed to begin individual intervention for Kim. A brief functional assessment session was conducted outside of the classroom to select an intervention (Figure 7.12). On the criterion skill (fact families), Kim performed the lowest in her class, scoring 13 digits correct in 2 minutes following class-wide intervention that had produced strong growth for her classmates. Her performance was unimproved with incentives. Reducing task difficulty improved her performance. Her instructional level was identified as sums to 10, and it was noted that she had trouble counting. Incentives at this level produced some improvement. Hence, Kim's intervention involved dropping down to a lower skill, emphasizing acquisition level instruction with brief fluency building at the end of the intervention and individualized incentives.

Then the intervention used guided practice, followed by cover-copy-compare followed by 3 minutes of flashcards using a ratio of 4 known items to 1 unknown item and an individualized reward system. A written protocol was provided to the teacher who agreed to conduct the intervention each day. The teacher was trained

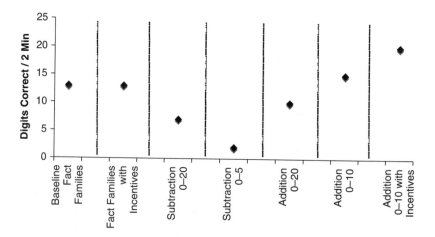

Figure 7.12 Functional Assessment Kim.

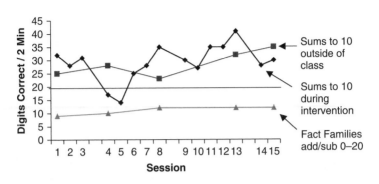

Figure 7.13 Kim's Intervention Progress.

to implement the intervention independently and then was provided with all necessary materials to run the intervention. Once per week an assessment probe was administered for sums to 10 (instructional level task) and a generalization probe for fact families addition and subtraction 0–20.

Kim showed no improved performance on the criterion skill and some progress on the targeted intervention skill. An integrity check was performed following the first week of intervention and the teacher scored 100%. Kim was observed to be actively engaged throughout the intervention session. Following week 2, the reward contingencies were adjusted to maximize motivation. Kim's error rate remained low during probe sessions indicating the task was of appropriate difficulty level. She showed growth during the intervention but it was not enough to meet the RtI success criterion. Kim was determined to have had a failed RtI. Her parents and teachers were invited to attend a multi-disciplinary team meeting at the school to review Kim's intervention progress and determine if a referral should be made for a comprehensive evaluation. Prior to the meeting, the team completed the checklist to evaluate decision accuracy under RtI. (See Appendix D.) There were no potential warning signs that error may have occurred in the RtI evaluation. (Screening measures were appropriate and correctly administered; class-wide interventions were actively being implemented with strong effects for the majority of students; Kim was one of a very small number of students remaining in the risk range despite increasingly intensive interventions being implemented with integrity; progress monitoring data were sensitive and available to evaluate intervention effects.) Following that meeting a referral was made, Kim was evaluated, and she was made eligible to receive services through special education under the category of SLD.

CASE EXAMPLE: SUCCESSFUL TIER 2 INTERVENTION AND A TIER 3 INTERVENTION FOR ONE STUDENT

This example occurred in an elementary school that served approximately 300 students in grades K through 5, approximately 40% of whom were eligible for a free or reduced-price lunch. Universal screening data were collected in September and indicated some class-wide problems. However, the median oral reading fluency (ORF) score for one particular 4th grade classroom was 73 words correct per minute (wcpm), which was well above the 25th percentile (68 wcpm) on a national norm. Thus, there was no class-wide problem for these 25 students, and the lowest 20% (5) were identified as needing a Tier 2 intervention. Students were identified by examining ORF data and scores from the Measures of Academic Progress (Northwest Evaluation Association, 2003).

Tier 2

The group consisted of four males and one female student; three were Caucasian, one was Hispanic, and one was Hmong. The data for the five students are listed in Table 7.1. The data indicated that although ORF was low, comprehension appeared to be a larger concern. Moreover, instruction in the fourth grade was heavily comprehension oriented but was more code based in third grade; these students did not experience significant difficulties in third grade. Thus, we assessed comprehension using grade-level MAZE probes (grade-level reading passage where every 7th word is deleted and the student is required to select the word to fill in the blank from three choices for each missing word during a timed silent reading interval) (see Table 7.1). We completed the analysis of data presented in Table 7.1 and concluded that we would focus on comprehension as our Tier 2 intervention. As shown in the table, all the students scored below

Table 7.1 Data for the Five Students

Student	ORF Baseline	ORF Post-Intervention	MAZE Baseline	MAZE Post-Intervention	MAZE Slope
Alex	65	113	09	23	.72
Chad	63	105	07	21	.71
Jenny	56	79	10	14	.18
Tim	61	103	08	25	.81
Rick	59	99	11	22	.60

Table 7.2 Form B: Analysis of Screening Data for Intervention and Prevention Planning for a Tier 2 Intervention

	Strategies	Main Idea	Inference
What Was Taught	Activate prior knowledge Predict Summarize Generate questions Clarify	Find the main idea, answer comprehension questions.	Determining relationships: Relationship stated. Relationship not stated. Generalize inference rules into reading passages
How It Was Taught	Each individual strategy was taught by: Modeling Working with the student Having the student work independently	Students previewed passage, wrote a prediction, and read passage. Main idea extraction was modeled. Students completed comprehension.	Explicit instruction: Inferring was taught. Students independently read passages and answered comprehension questions with support from interventionist. Interventionist discussed answers using corrective feedback on errors.

Source: Based on Scholin, Haegele, Limm, and Burns (2009).

the 25th percentile for ORF and MAZE (9 correct responses per minute [crpm]; Hosp, Hosp, & Howell, 2008) during the October assessments.

As shown in Table 7.2, we focused on comprehension strategies, extracting the main idea and inferences. We met with the students three times each week for 30 minutes each session to deliver the intervention. We used reading passages taken from the curriculum as the intervention stimuli, and used explicit instruction of each strategy using the model, lead, and test format. Thus, the interventionist would first model the strategy using a think-aloud method and then work with the students to perform the strategy together. Once the students appeared to understand the strategy, they were asked to perform the strategy independently on a new passage. Progress was monitored with weekly MAZE assessments.

The intervention began at the end of October and continued until one month after returning from winter break. The students made progress throughout the interventions, and all but one scored above the 50th percentile on the final MAZE assessment in February (18 crpm; Hosp et al., 2008). Moreover, Fuchs

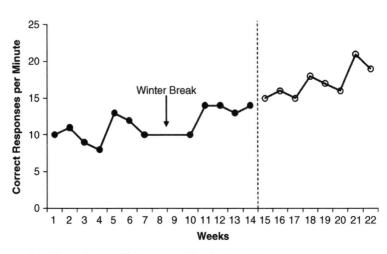

Figure 7.14 Jenny's MAZE Progress Monitoring Data.

and Fuchs (2004) indicated that .40 crpm per week was an acceptable criterion to which MAZE growth can be compared, and all but one student exceeded that criterion. Thus, the Tier 2 intervention ended by teaching the four students for whom the intervention was successful how to complete graphic organizers and continuing to monitor their progress on a weekly basis. However, the intervention was judged as not successful for Jenny, and additional analyses were conducted. (See Figure 7.14.)

Tier 3

Jenny was a Hmong female who exhibited difficulties with both ORF and comprehension. We then hypothesized that two difficulties could be interfering with her reading. First, we were concerned that vocabulary may be an issue, given that she was an English-language learner. We reviewed recent language assessments (including measures of receptive vocabulary), all of which fell within the average range. Thus, we concluded that she likely had acceptable vocabulary to learn reading but decided to continue vocabulary-building activities with her. Second, we hypothesized that fluency was an issue with her because her ORF was low and that she could not comprehend her reading because she did not read fluently enough. We then conducted a curriculum-based assessment for instructional design (Gickling & Havertape, 1981) using grade-level material and found that she read between 65 and 80 wcpm but read only between 78% and 88% of the words correctly.

Given Jenny's low fluency and accuracy while reading, we also screened her phonetic skills with the word attack subtest of the Woodcock Reading Mastery Test. Her age-based standard score of 90 (25th percentile) indicated that she could successfully decode words to an acceptable level. Thus, our intervention consisted of teaching her words from a fourth-grade word list using incremental rehearsal (IR; Tucker, 1989) and having her practice blending sounds into words using various word sorts (Joseph, 2000). We again met with her three times each week for approximately 30 minutes each session. As shown in Figure 7.14, Jenny's MAZE scores increased after the intervention changed. Her ORF scores increased from 79 to 107 wcpm over 8 weeks and from 78% to 88% correct to 94% correct. However, comprehension increased at .65 crpm per week despite our intervention's focus on reading fluency. Moreover, her final MAZE score was slightly over the 50th percentile. At this point we determined that the intervention was successful and Jenny was again placed into a Tier 2 intervention small group for reading.

CASE EXAMPLE: IMPLEMENTATION INTEGRITY OF PROBLEM-SOLVING TEAM

Problem-solving teams (PSTs) are important aspects of most RtI models. Grade-level teams are the decision-making bodies within RtI, and PSTs do not come into play until Tier 3. Grade-level teams interpret universal screening data, examine progress monitoring data from Tiers 2 and 3, and determine when a student should be referred for a specific learning disability (SLD) identification evaluation. Of course, all of these decisions are made in consultation with someone with expertise in data management. Generally speaking, two professionals in each elementary school building make up a data management team. Those two professionals have expertise in data consumption, spreadsheet software, and similar areas. One representative of the data management team attends grade-level team meetings when data are discussed (e.g., immediately after universal screening data are collected or the once-a-month meeting where the grade-level team discusses progress monitoring data) to facilitate a conversation about the questions in Table 7.3.

Once the grade-level team examines Tier 2 progress monitoring data and concludes that a student needs a more intensive intervention, they then refer the student to the building's PST. The PST then conducts an in-depth problem analysis to develop individualized interventions and determines the progress monitoring plan for the student. This process is critical to most RtI models but is rarely implemented correctly. Next we present an example of how the PST

Table 7.3 Questions for Grade-Level Team Data Meeting

1. Are there any class-wide problems?
2. If there are no class-wide problems, which students need a Tier 2 intervention?
3. What data are needed to decide which tier 2 intervention to use with each student?
4. Is the Tier 2 intervention working for each individual student receiving one?
5. Should we refer any students to the problem-solving team?
6. Is the Tier 3 intervention working for each individual student receiving one?
7. Are there any students whom we should refer for a special education evaluation?

process was poorly implemented but was then reformed to better address student needs.

School

The school in which this example occurred was a K–8 building that served 605 students, about half of whom were eligible for a free or reduced price lunch. The PST met whenever there were students to discuss and included these standing members on the team: the student's referring teacher, the school psychologist, the social worker, a speech and language therapist, an occupational therapist, the physical education teacher, and a special education teacher. Other school personnel, including the principal, attended meetings inconsistently. The team discussed two or three children at each meeting, which were held in the social worker's office and lasted between 45 minutes and 1 hour each.

The school collected universal screening data three times each year and addressed class-wide problems appropriately. However, their Tier 2 intervention system was just starting, and many students eventually were referred to the PST. Listed in Table 7.4 are the percentages of the student body that were referred to each aspect of the RtI model. Approximately 20% of the students received a Tier 2 intervention, which was consistent with recommendations (Batsche et al., 2005). However, approximately half of those students were referred to Tier 3, and 80% of those students were eventually referred to special education. Moreover, approximately 63% of the students who were tested for a special education disability were actually identified with a disability. Although the school seemed to address class-wide problems adequately, Tiers 2 and 3 were clearly not working.

Intervention

We began by observing the Tier 2 and were quickly able to almost double the number of students for whom the interventions were successful. Fully explaining

Table 7.4 Percentage of Students Referred for Tier 2, Tier 3, and Special Education

Students	% of Student Body before PST Feedback	% of Student Body after PST Feedback
Receiving a Tier 2 intervention	Approximately 20%	Approximately 20%
Receiving a Tier 3 intervention	Approximately 10%	Approximately 7%
Referred for a special education evaluation	Approximately 8%	Approximately 2%
Placed into special education	Approximately 5%	Between 1.5% and 2%

the process within Tier 2 goes beyond the scope of this example, but essentially we observed the interventions using the observation form included in the supplemental materials for this book provided in the appendix, grouped children more carefully based on data, and more closely targeted the interventions.

The PST was about to disband out of frustration and exhaustion when we began working with it. We started by observing the PSTs each week using the checklist created by Burns, Wiley, and Viglietta (2008), the items for which are included in Table 7.5. As can be seen from the data, most items were observed less than two-thirds of the time, and critically important activities (e.g., baseline

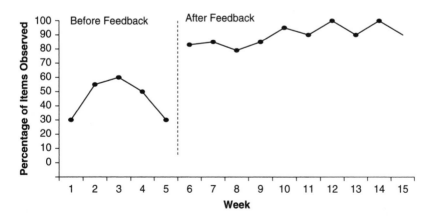

Figure 7.15 Percentage of Problem-Solving Team Implementation Items Observed.

data were presented, and specific implementation plan developed) rarely occurred.

Because of the low implementation and somewhat dismal outcomes, we focused on the PST implementation. We began by meeting with the PST at the beginning of the school year for 15 minutes. During that time we reviewed the PST purpose and process with the PST members and provided each member with a manual and a book chapter (Burns et al., 2008) about PST implementation. We then provided weekly performance feedback (PFB) that was modeled after Noell et al. (2005). We completed the PST Implementation Checklist detailed in Table 7.5 at each PST meeting, graphed the number of items observed, distributed an updated graph each week to the PST members at the next meeting, discussed individual items to reinforce correct implementation for some and pointed out those items that were omitted, and brainstormed ways to better address the missed items.

As can be seen in Figure 7.15, the implementation integrity of the PST process increased immediately after providing PFB, and the implementation of individual items also increased (Table 7.5). The number of students referred for a special education evaluation from Tier 3 was reduced by about half, which was less than

Table 7.5 Percentage of Items Observed at Problem-Solving Team Meetings

Item	Baseline	With Feedback
Team meets on a weekly basis	100%	100%
Request for Assistance Form (RAF) is used provide data before the meeting	93%	100%
The RAF is brief but provides adequate information about the problem	100%	100%
Documentation of consultant meeting with teacher prior to PST meeting	63%	95%
Baseline data are presented	25%	93%
Data are objective and empirical	66%	85%
Selected interventions are research based	25%	85%
Selected intervention is directly linked to assessment data	38%	100%
Start with interventions that have a high probability of success	13%	75%

Table 7.5 (continued)

Item	Baseline	With Feedback
Consulting personnel assist with implementation of intervention	35%	80%
Team develops specific implementation plan with teacher	13%	90%
Parent information is discussed	87%	100%
Data collection plan is developed to monitor effectiveness and progress	45%	90%
Monitoring data are objective, empirical, and directly linked to the problem	40%	75%
A plan is developed to assess implementation integrity of the intervention	00%	50%
Follow-up consultation is scheduled between teacher and one PST member	50%	95%
Follow-up meeting is scheduled	50%	100%
A case documentation form is used to track the team's activities	100%	100%
The building principal or administrative designee is present at the meeting	20%	88%
PST members have designated roles (e.g., note taker, discussion facilitator)	00%	100%

one-third of students receiving a Tier 3 intervention. Our hope is that this number will continue to decline, but it was down to approximately 2% of the student population. Moreover, approximately 90% of the students who were referred for a special education evaluation were identified with a disability, which was an increase from 63% and represented a more efficient use of resources.

The performance feedback continued after our involvement ended but was then conducted through PST self-assessments each week. Although there was still plenty of room for improvement, the PST became the essential part of Tier 3 that it was designed to be.

Appendix A

Evaluation of Screening Data Accuracy

Grade	Teacher Name	Screening Skill	Screening Integrity	Class-wide Problem?		Grade-wide Problem?	
				Reading	Math	Reading	Math
Grade 1	Teacher A						
	Teacher B						
	Teacher C						
	Teacher D						
Grade 2	Teacher E						
	Teacher F						
	Teacher G						
	Teacher H						
Grade 3	Teacher I						
	Teacher J						
	Teacher K						
	Teacher L						
Grade 4	Teacher M						
	Teacher N						
	Teacher O						
	Teacher P						

(*continued*)

Grade	Teacher Name	Screening Skill	Screening Integrity	Class-wide Problem?		Grade-wide Problem?	
				Reading	Math	Reading	Math
Grade 5	Teacher Q						
	Teacher R						
	Teacher S						
	Teacher T						

Appendix B

Analysis of Screening Data for Intervention and Prevention Planning

Step 1	Rule-out class-wide problem. (Print class-wide and grade-wide graphs with criterion reference.)⟶	Proceed to individual assessment and intervention as needed.	
Step 2	If class-wide problem is not ruled out, consider . . . ⟶	Was measurement task appropriate?	
		Was measurement correctly administered?	
		Common features of classes apparent?⟶	By grade?
			By content?
			By particular teachers?
			Are students being tracked?
			Demographic features of students?
		Look backward.⟶	Prerequisite skills mastered?
			Rapid increase in content difficulty or expectations for learning?
		Look forward.⟶	Deficits apparent at subsequent grade levels?
Step 3	PRIORITIZE intervention targets.	Consider patterns and prioritize (by grade, by content, by demographics, others).	
Step 4	COORDINATE efforts to . . .	Repair existing problems.	
		Prevent future problems.	
Step 5	EVALUATE solutions.	Monitor % of class-wide problems.	
		% of grade-wide problems.	
		% of students below criterion on screening (by demographic features).	

Appendix C

Troubleshooting Instructional Basics

Troubleshooting Instructional Basics Checklist			
Troubleshooting Instructional Foundations	**Yes**	**No**	**Solutions if "No" Is Checked**
Adequate materials are available to facilitate instruction.			Ensure instructional materials available. Ensure student assessment system is matched to instruction and is available for all students with data-tracking software.
Clearly defined essential skills in sequence.			Review standards to prioritize most important skills, specify sequence for instruction, ensure essential skills are taught to mastery
Calendar for teaching skills.			Specify when essential skills will be taught and by which date they will be mastered for the entire year. Work with teachers to follow the instructional calendar to ensure all skills are taught to mastery.
Adequate instructional time devoted to instruction, practice with feedback, and guided application.			Review time available for instruction each day in the classroom. Make adjustments based on prioritized essential skills and prioritized intervention targets.
Professional development activities provide for coaching and feedback to teacher implementation efforts.			Review professional development resources to ensure a keen focus on prioritized intervention targets.
Troubleshooting Instructional Interaction	**Yes**	**No**	**Solutions if "No" Is Checked**
Task presentation clear with correct and incorrect examples of responding demonstrated for students.			Include observations in classrooms as part of personnel review.
Use of sufficient cues to provide guided practice correctly completing task during instruction until students can accurately complete the task (100% accuracy untimed).			Include observations in classrooms as part of personnel review.

(continued)

Troubleshooting Instructional Interaction	Yes	No	Solutions if "No" Is Checked
Pacing of instruction matched to student need.			Integrate student assessment with instructional planning. Ensure software available to organize student learning data, and provide professional development to assist teachers in translating student learning data to more effective instruction.
Degree of feedback matched to student competence.			Integrate student assessment with instructional planning. Ensure software available to organize student learning data, and provide professional development to assist teachers in translating student learning data to more effective instruction.
Skills introduced according to calendar of instruction.			Build a calendar of instruction that specifies when essential skills will be taught and by which date they will be mastered. Ensure a system for assessing student learning is in place. Assess student learning at routine intervals to ensure that skills are established by specified dates for most students. Link these skills and dates to universal screening measurement selection.
Student mastery of taught skills is assessed and opportunities are provided for additional instruction or enrichment as needed.			Ensure there is a master calendar providing time for supplemental instruction (e.g., via Tier 2 and Tier 3). Ensure most students master skills according to instructional calendar.
Students are actively engaged.			Check via direct observation. If engagement is low, troubleshoot task difficulty. (Tasks may be a poor match with student capability.) Actively address weak skills with class-wide intervention. Minimize transition times (less than 2 minutes per transition) and time devoted to noninstructional activities in class. Emphasize active student responding with feedback and incentives for high-quality work production.
Time devoted to noninstructional activity is minimized (e.g., transition time).			Check via direct observation. All transitions should be less than 2 minutes. Initiate a transition routine intervention to reduce transition times due to their direct and devastating cost to instructional time and student learning outcomes.
Instructional time emphasizes practice with feedback.			Include observations in classroom as part of personnel review. Devote professional development activities to increasing active student responding.

Appendix D

Dealing with Potential Sources of Error in RtI Decision Making

CHECKLIST TO EVALUATE TECHNICAL ADEQUACY FOR RTI IMPLEMENTATIONS AND DECISION MAKING	
RtI Component	**Check any of the following that may apply:**
Screen All Students	_____Nonvalidated tool selected for use.
	_____Scores inconsistent over short intervals of time where instruction would not be expected to have caused much change.
	If yes, STOP. Measure may not be reliable, valid, or sensitive.
	_____Digital timers not used.
	_____Scored screening protocols unavailable.
	If yes, STOP. Measure may have been incorrectly administered.
	_____Any number of children for whom no decision has been made after 30 days.
	_____Children below criterion at screening who did not receive intervention.
	_____Children with failed RtI who are not referred for further assessment.
	_____Children with successful RtI who are referred for further assessment.
	If yes, STOP. Data may not have been correctly interpreted.
Determine Risk	_____High numbers of false positive errors.
	If yes, STOP. Cut point may not be efficient. Consider "successive" hurdles to improve efficiency.
	_____Use of normative data only.

	If yes, STOP. Cut point may not be accurate. Benchmark criterion should be included.
	_____Children above criterion receiving intervention.
	_____Children below criterion not receiving intervention.
	_____Too few students receive intervention (< 10% of students receiving Tier 2 or 3 intervention).
	_____Delay to intervention implementation (>30 days from initial risk decision to intervention implementation).
	If yes, STOP. Cut point may not have been correctly applied.
Identify Patterns	_____School-wide, grade-wide, and class-wide performance problems apparent on consecutive screenings.
	If yes, STOP. Data need to be examined to identify system targets.
	_____Disaggregated findings unavailable.
	If yes, STOP. Data need to be evaluated to ensure equity of achievement.
	_____Screening <3 times per year.
	If yes, STOP. Screening should occur at least 3 times per year.
Link to Resource Allocation Decisions	_____Greater than 20% of students performed below criterion on consecutive screenings.
	If yes, STOP. School-wide and grade-wide learning problems should be assessed and addressed.
	_____Children in risk range on consecutive screenings.
	If yes, STOP. Intervention may not have occurred as planned.
	_____Children who received supplemental instruction remain in risk range on consecutive screenings.
	If yes, STOP. Interventions were not tracked to ensure effects.
Determine Tier 2 or 3 Interventions	_____Tier 3 interventions implemented for greater than 10% of screened population.
	If yes, STOP. Tier 2 interventions should be implemented.
Select and Implement Intervention	_____Delay to intervention outcome decision (>30 days from intervention implementation to intervention outcome decision).
	_____No intervention protocols available, no integrity data available.

(continued)

	_____Tier 2 interventions unsuccessful for greater than 20% of those exposed to Tier 2 intervention (10% of screened population).
	_____Tier 3 interventions unsuccessful for greater than 10% of those exposed to intervention (5% of screened population).
	If yes, STOP. Intervention implementation integrity must be directly assessed and ensured.
Evaluate Intervention Effects	_____Tier 2 interventions unsuccessful for greater than 20% of those exposed to Tier 2 intervention (10% of screened population).
	_____Tier 3 interventions unsuccessful for greater than 10% of those exposed to intervention (5% of screened population).
	If yes, STOP. Progress monitoring data may not be reliable, valid, or sensitive.
	_____Highly variable data points from week to week.
	If yes, STOP. Check accuracy of administration of progress monitoring measures.
	_____More than 1 week between progress monitoring data points.
	_____Fewer than 3 progress monitoring data points.
	If yes, STOP. Increase the frequency of progress monitoring data collection.
Troubleshoot Intervention Effects	_____No integrity data available.
	If yes, STOP. Integrity must be directly measured.
	_____Integrity data suggest implementation did not occur correctly and interventionist was not retrained with performance feedback follow-up documented.
	If yes, STOP. Intervention implementation integrity was not sufficient.
	_____Highly variable child performance during intervention may signal integrity problem or motivation problem that requires troubleshooting.
	_____Poor growth may signal need to adjust intervention by reducing task difficulty and increasing antecedent support for correct responding and frequency/immediacy of corrective feedback.
	_____Strong growth but below-criterion performance may indicate need to advance difficulty level of materials, further support fluent skill development through use of incentives and maximizing opportunities to respond.
	_____Poor generalization may signal the need for antecedent supports and opportunities to practice generalizing the training skill, increasing task variation, and fading of supports to more natural conditions.

	If yes, STOP. Intervention should be adjusted to maximize effects (materials too challenging or too easy, individualized rewards not provided, corrective feedback not matched to student need).
Judge Intervention Outcome	_____Many failed responses to intervention (incidence greater than 5% of screened population).
	If yes, STOP. Intervention integrity may not have been adequate, causing false positive identification errors.
	_____Fewer than 10 consecutive intervention sessions implemented with integrity following troubleshooting.
	If yes, STOP. Intervention was incomplete.
	_____Highly variable data patterns.
	If yes, STOP. No troubleshooting of the intervention occurred.
	_____Children with successful RtI referred for evaluation.
	_____Children with unsuccessful RtI not referred for evaluation.
	_____Children without a decision in 30 days.
	If yes, STOP. Judgment was incorrect (does not correspond to data collected).
Link to Resource Allocation Decisions	_____Children with unsuccessful RtI not referred for evaluation.
	If yes, STOP. Those with unsuccessful RtI should be referred for further assessment and/or comprehensive evaluation.
	_____Children with successful RtI referred for evaluation.
	If yes, STOP. Children with a successful RtI should not be referred for further assessment.
	_____Graph showing student performance relative to classmates and some criterion, graph showing performance during intervention, and intervention protocol not included in child's permanent folder.
	If yes, STOP. The RtI outcome should be shared and documented via brief teacher and parent meeting, resource plan for the student, and assessment and intervention data included in file.

Appendix E

MONITORING TIER 2 INTERVENTION

Generic Tier 2 Intervention Observation Protocol

Item	Observed	
The Tier II intervention is:		
Implemented or supervised by a qualified teacher with appropriate expertise.	Yes	No
Delivered to a small group of students (e.g., about 5 in elementary school, 8 for middle school, and 10 for high school).	Yes	No
Implemented 3 to 5 times/week in 20- to 30-minute sessions.	Yes	No
Implementation time is NOT part of core instruction time.	Yes	No
Designed to last at least 8 weeks.	Yes	No
Individual student progress monitored with a fluency-based measure at least twice each month.	Yes	No
Intervention is targeted but consistent with core curriculum.	Yes	No
Consists of instructional methods with a sound scientific base and demonstrated effectiveness.	Yes	No

Source: Based on Burns et al. (2006).

Appendix F

Screening Integrity Protocol

☐ A set of content-controlled/standard materials was used to conduct the screening.

☐ The screened skill reflects a grade-level skill, and the teacher had an opportunity to give input on the skill selected for screening.

☐ The teacher followed scripted standardized administration procedures to administer the probe.

☐ The teacher used a digital timer to time the screening measure administration.

☐ All students began working when directed to do so and stopped working when the timer beeped.

☐ Total number of steps observed/divided by 5 and multiplied by 100% is the percent integrity score for screening.

AUTHORS' NOTE

ROC

False positive and false negative errors are inversely related. Detecting more true positives (or decreasing false negative errors) necessarily comes at a cost to increased false positive errors. Receiver Operating Characteristics (ROC) analyses can be used to identify the score or cutpoint that provides the best balance between types of errors (failing to detect students who should be detected and over-detecting students). The ROC visually represents the utility of the full range of potential cutscores. For each possible score on the "test" measure, the ROC plots the true positive rate (sensitivity) on the y-axis and false positive rate on the x-axis (1-specificity). The curve begins at the 0, 0 coordinate on the graph which is the strictest possible cutscore where all cases are negative and ends at the 1, 1 coordinate which is the most lenient possible cutscore where all cases are positive. The number of datapoints on the ROC curve is the total number of unique scores less one. So if in a dataset of 200 cases, 200 scores are obtained ranging from 50 to 190, then the curve begins at 49 (no false positive errors because all cases are coded negative at this score because no one scored 49 or lower) and ends at 191 (no false negative errors because all cases are coded positive because all cases scored lower than 191). Because the number of datapoints on the ROC curve includes only unique scores, the highest possible datapoints on the ROC (or scores considered as potential cutscores) is $(141 - 1)$ or 140 possible datapoints if every score occurred at least once in the dataset.

To facilitate interpretation of the ROC, a perfectly diagonal trendline represents equivalent false positive and true positive rates (indicating no diagnostic utility). To interpret the ROC, users identify the highest true positive rate (highest vertical point) that is associated with the lowest false positive rate (closest to the y-axis). The score associated with this point on the trendline offers the best balance between sensitivity and specificity. Area Under the Curve can be computed to reflect how accurate the ROC is at separating true positives from false positives. Given a randomly selected person who truly has the condition the test is intended to diagnose and a randomly selected person who truly does not have the condition, the Area Under the Curve estimate is the probability that the diagnostic test will rate the patient with the condition as having higher suspicion for the condition than the patient without the condition. The chance diagonal representing the point at which the false positive rate is equal to the true positive rate has an Area Under the Curve value of .50. The benefit of the Area Under the Curve estimate is that it can be compared across and within studies to identify diagnostic measures and procedures that have the greatest accuracy or value in separating true positives from false positives. Recall that positive and negative predictive power values are nearly never comparable across studies due to their susceptibility to changing prevalence rates. Also, sensitivity and specificity are only comparable when the gold standard measure and cutpoint is the same and the samples come from the same population. A limitation of the Area Under the Curve estimate is that it is estimated based upon all possible thresholds including those that would not be used in practice. For example, the Area Under the Curve estimate considers all of the area under the ROC curve and this includes potential cutscores that are at the very low or very high end of the score distribution, which would never really be useful cutpoints in practice. As an alternative to the Area Under the Curve, the Partial Area Under the Curve may be used to more accurately reflect the test's utility in separating true positives and false positives for the range of scores that might actually be used as cutscores in practice (scores at a given false positive rate, e.g., false positive rate of less than 10%).

Clinicians can readily and visually use the ROC curve to consider the trade-offs in sensitivity versus specificity for various cutpoints to identify the best cutpoint. But cutpoint selection need not necessarily be the one that provides the perfect trade-off in false and true positives. For example, cutpoint selection might be influenced by the costs associated with making a false negative error (failing to detect a true positive). Where the cost of failing to detect a true positive carries very negative consequences, a higher false-positive rate may be tolerated in favor of ensuring fewer false negative errors. On the other hand, it is feasible that in some cases the cost associated with a false-positive error may be higher (e.g., followed by intrusive, painful, and costly assessment or treatment procedures) than those associated with making a false-negative error. It is worth noting that no measure and cutscore will be perfect. Errors are to be expected and failure to consider the values, priorities, and costs associated with error types is a major mistake in setting cutscores. RtI research is not immune to this vulnerability. Consequences of different decision errors at each stage of RtI decision making have not been well-specified or well-researched.

ROC analysis has been widely researched and used in the health sciences (e.g., to establish cutpoints or values for interpreting chemical tests, for interpreting radiographic studies). One very promising finding from the field of radiology involves the multiple-reader multiple-case design. This approach recognizes the subjective nature of interpreting radiographic studies and generates a range of ROC curves arising from trained interpreters. The purpose of this approach has been well-articulated by Obuchowski (2) as not intending to average out the ROCs to generate a "consensus" curve that would then be interpreted in setting cutpoints and determining diagnostic efficiency of a test, but rather to characterize the range of curves and associated cutscores that are possible under typical conditions. This multiple-reader multiple-case approach is directly relevant to educational psychology. An exciting extension of the multiple-reader multiple-case approach so prevalent in Radiology would be to examine and quantify the effects of measurement parameters (e.g., task difficulty, use of a median score versus a single score at screening) to quantify decision value in RtI. For example, decisions may be influenced systematically by reading scores that differ across passage types (even when the passages are assumed to be equivalent). As mentioned in Chapter 1, nuanced risk models may evolve where risk factors could be combined in additive fashion to enhance overall prediction (e.g., reading fluency score plus age of child plus free or reduced lunch status). Combined ROC curves could be generated to characterize the utility of the combined test variables. Whereas ROC analyses are valuable in RtI implementations, allowing districts and schools to empirically identify the cutpoints for decision making that will best advance student outcomes at the lowest cost, several limitations should be considered. Cutpoint scores identified through ROC analyses are only as meaningful as the conditions under which the data were collected. Users must attend to the quality of data collection and choose assessment tasks that are meaningful for the decision the scores are intended to inform. Cutscores identified through ROC analysis should be cross-validated on subsequent samples to ensure that the diagnostic accuracy estimates replicate (Jenkins et al., 2007). Users should consider the type of decision that the data will inform, consider the costs of false positive versus false negative errors for that decision and identify the cutpoint that provides the best decision accuracy that also comes at the lowest cost. Users should also consume research findings in a critical fashion concerning ROC analysis, applying the criteria raised by Meehl and Rosen (1955), that is, even very accurate diagnostic tests can become wholly unimpressive in high-prevalence and low-prevalence conditions. Given that SLD diagnosis is anticipated to be a low-prevalence condition, data that will inform such a decision are particularly susceptible in this regard. ROC analysis findings are highly dependent on the selected cutscore for the gold standard measure as well. In education and psychology, there are no real gold standard criteria, there are only outcome measures that we think reflect the desired outcome. These measures often yield continuous scores that must be converted to categories. The placement of the cutpoint for these measures can influence the ROC and diagnostic accuracy estimates. Where Area Under the Curve values drive the decisions about where to place cutpoints, it is a definite risk that some researchers may play with criteria on both the diagnostic measure and the outcome measure until the values look strong. This approach is analogous to the tail wagging the dog. Consumers of ROC data should critically examine the degree to which the outcome measures were meaningful, the cutscores were functional, and the data were adequately collected. Several scholars have cautioned that ROC analyses may overestimate sensitivity and specificity, particularly in studies involving sample sizes below 200 (Leeflang, Moons, Reitsma, & Zwinderman, 1). These authors demonstrated via simulated data the systematic and detrimental effects of small sample sizes and prevalence rates diverging from 50-50 (50% of sample with the condition, 50% without). One of the suggestions for dealing with systematic overestimation of sensitivity and specificity was to use a prespecified cutscore based on existing research (i.e., avoiding the ROC altogether).

REFERENCES

Leeflang, M. M. G., Moons, K. G. M., Reitsma, J. B., & Zwinderman, A. H. (2008). Bias in sensitivity and specificity caused by data-driven selection of optimal cutoff values: Mechanisms, magnitude, and solutions. *Clinical Chemistry, 54,* 729–737.

Obuchowski, N. A. (2005). Fundamentals of clinical research for radiologists: ROC analysis. *American Journal of Roentgenology, 184,* 364–372.

REFERENCES

Aaron, P. G. (1997). The impending demise of the discrepancy formula. *Review of Educational Research, 67*, 461–502.

Adams, M. J. (1990). *Beginning to read: Thinking and learning about print.* Cambridge, MA: MIT Press.

Aimsweb (2008). *Progress monitoring and RtI system.* Bloomington, MN: Pearson.

Alexander, A. M. (2006, March 28). Latest legal issues impacting general education interventions. Workshop presented at the National Association of School Psychologists meeting, Anaheim, CA.

Algozzine, B., & Ysseldyke, J. E. (1982). Classification decisions in learning disabilities. *Educational and Psychological Research, 2*, 117–129.

Algozzine, B., & Ysseldyke, J. E. (1983). Learning disabilities as a subset of school failure: The over-sophistication of a concept. *Exceptional Children, 50*, 242–246.

Algozzine, B., Ysseldyke, J. E., & Christenson, S. (1983). An analysis of the incidence of special class placement: The masses are burgeoning. *Journal of Special Education, 17*, 141–147.

American Educational Research Association, American Psychological Association, and the National Council on Measurement in Education (1999). *Standards for educational and psychological testing.* Washington, DC: American Educational Research Association.

Anastasi, A., & Urbina, S. (1997). *Psychological testing* (7th ed). Upper Saddle River, NJ: Prentice Hall.

Ardoin, S. P., & Christ, T. J. (2008). Evaluating curriculum-based measurement slope estimates using data from triannual universal screenings. *School Psychology Review, 37*, 109–125.

Ardoin, S. P., & Daly, E. J., III (2007). Introduction to the special series: Close encounters of the instructional kind—How the instructional hierarchy is shaping instructional research 30 years later. *Journal of Behavioral Education, 16*, 1–6.

Ardoin, S. P., Witt, J. C., Suldo, S. M., Koenig, J., McDonald, E., & Smith, L. (2004). The response in response to intervention: Evaluating the sensitivity of curriculum-based measurement to intervention effects. *School Psychology Review, 33*, 218–233.

Bakeman, R., & Gottman, J. M. (1986). *Observing interaction: An introduction to sequential analysis.* New York: Cambridge University Press.

Bahr, M. W., & Fuchs, D. (1991). Are teachers' perceptions of difficult-to-teach students racially biased? *School Psychology Review, 20*, 99–609.

Barnett, D. W., Bell, S. H., Gilkey, C. M., Lentz, F. E., Graden, J. L., Stone, C. M., et al. (1999). The promise of meaningful eligibility determination: Functional intervention-based multifactored preschool evaluation. *Journal of Special Education, 33*, 112–124.

Barnett, D. W., Daly, E. J., III, Jones, K. M., & Lentz, F. E., Jr. (2004). Response to intervention: Empirically-based special service decisions from increasing and decreasing intensity single case designs. *Journal of Special Education, 38*, 66–79.

Batsche, G., Elliott, J., Graden, J. L., Grimes, J., Kovaleski, J. F., Prasse, D., et al. (2005). *Response to intervention policy considerations and implementation*. Reston, VA: National Association of State Directors of Special Education.

Batsche, G., Kavale, K. A., & Kovaleski, J. F. (2006). Competing views: A dialogue on response to intervention. *Assessment for Effective Intervention, 32*, 6–19.

Berninger, V. W., Abbott, R. D., Vermeulen, K., & Fulton, C. M. (2006). Paths to reading comprehension in at-risk second-grade readers. *Journal of Learning Disabilities, 39*, 334–351.

Betts, E. A. (1946). *Foundations of reading instructions with emphasis on differentiated guidance*. New York: American Book Company.

Bloom, B. S., Hastings, J. T., & Madaus, G. F. (1971). *Handbook on formative and summative evaluation of student learning*. New York: McGraw-Hill.

Bollman, K. A., Silberglitt, B., & Gibbons, K. A. (2007). The St. Croix River Education District model: Incorporating systems-level organization and a multi-tiered problem-solving process for intervention delivery. In S. R. Jimerson, M. K. Burns, & A. M. VanDerHeyden (Eds.), *Handbook of response to intervention: The science and practice of assessment and intervention* (pp. 319–330). New York: Springer.

Botvin, G. (2004). Advancing prevention science and practice: Challenges, critical issues, and future directions. *Prevention Science, 5*, 69–72.

Bransford, J., & Stein, B. (1984). The ideal problem solver: A guide for improving thinking, learning and creativity. San Francisco: W. H. Freeman.

Burns, M. K. (2004). Empirical analysis of drill ratio research: Refining the instructional level for drill tasks. *Remedial and Special Education, 25*, 167–175.

Burns, M. K. (2007). Using curriculum-based assessment to match instruction and skill: Implications for response to intervention. *School Psychology Quarterly, 22*, 297–313.

Burns, M. K. (2007). RtI WILL fail, unless . . . *Communiqué, 35*, 38–40.

Burns, M. K. (2008). Response to intervention at the secondary level. *Principal Leadership: High School Edition, 8*, 12–15.

Burns, M. K., Appleton, J. J., & Stehouwer, J. D. (2005). Meta-analytic review of response-to-intervention research: Examining field-based and research-implemented models. *Journal of Psychoeducational Assessment, 23*, 381–394.

Burns, M. K., Christ, T. J., Boice, C., & Szadokierski, I. (in press). Special education in an RtI model: Addressing unique learning needs. In T. A. Glover & S. Vaughn (Eds.), *Response to intervention: Empowering all students to learn—A critical account of the science and practice*. New York: Guilford.

Burns, M. K., Dean, V. J., & Klar, S. (2004). Using curriculum-based assessment in the responsiveness to intervention diagnostic model for learning disabilities. *Assessment for Effective Intervention, 29*, 47–56.

Burns, M. K., Deno, S. L., & Jimerson, S. R. (2007). Toward a unified response-to-intervention model. In S. R. Jimerson, M. K. Burns, & A. M. VanDerHeyden (Eds.), *Handbook of response to intervention: The science and practice of assessment and intervention* (pp. 428–440). New York: Springer.

Burns, M. K., & Gibbons, K. (2008). *Response to intervention implementation in elementary and secondary schools: Procedures to assure scientific-based practices*. New York: Routledge.

Burns, M. K., Peters, R., & Noell, G. H. (2008). Using performance feedback to enhance the implementation integrity of the problem-solving team process. *Journal of School Psychology, 46*, 537–550.

Burns, M. K., Scholin, S. E., Kosciolek, S., & Livingston, J. (in press). Reliability of decision-making frameworks for response to intervention for reading. *Journal of Psychoeducational Assessment.*

Burns, M. K., & Senesac, B. K. (2005). Comparison of dual discrepancy criteria for diagnosis of unresponsiveness to intervention. *Journal of School Psychology, 43,* 393–406.

Burns, M. K., & Symington, T. (2002). A meta-analysis of prereferral intervention teams: Systemic and student outcomes. *Journal of School Psychology, 40,* 437–447.

Burns, M. K., Tilly, W. D., III, Gresham, F., Telzrow, C. F., Shapiro, E. S., & Kovaleski, J. F. (2006). Response-to-intervention debate: Using data over dogma. *Communiqué, 34,* 5–6.

Burns, M. K., & VanDerHeyden, A. M. (2006). Using response to intervention to assess learning disabilities: Introduction to the special series. *Assessment for Effective Intervention, 32,* 3–5.

Burns, M. K., VanDerHeyden, A. M., & Boice, C. H. (2008). Best practices in delivery intensive academic interventions. In A. Thomas & J. Grimes (Eds.), *Best practices in school psychology* (5th ed., pp. 1151–1162). Bethesda, MD: National Association of School Psychologists.

Burns, M. K., VanDerHeyden, A. M., & Jiban, C. (2006). Assessing the instructional level for mathematics: A comparison of methods. *School Psychology Review, 35,* 401–418.

Burns, M. K., Wagner, A., & Jacob, S. (2008). Ethical and legal issues associated with using response-to-intervention to assess learning disabilities. *Journal of School Psychology, 46,* 263–279.

Burns, M. K., & Wagner, D. (2008). Determining an effective intervention within a brief experimental analysis for reading: A meta-analytic review. *School Psychology Review, 37,* 126–136.

Burns, M. K., Wiley, H. I., & Viglietta, E. (2008). Best practices in facilitating problem-solving teams. In A. Thomas & J. Grimes (Eds.), *Best practices in school psychology* (5th ed., pp. 1633–1644). Bethesda, MD: National Association of School Psychologists.

Burns, M. K., & Ysseldyke, J. E. (2005). Questions about responsiveness-to-intervention implementation: Seeking answers from existing models. *California School Psychologist, 10,* 9–20.

Campbell, D. T., & Fiske, D. W. (1959). Convergent and discriminant validation by the multitrait-multimethod matrix. *Psychological Bulletin, 56,* 81–105.

Center for Teaching and Learning. (2008). *Dynamic indicators of early literacy skills data system.* Eugene, OR: University of Oregon Center on Teaching and Learning.

Chall, J. S. (1983). *Stages of reading development.* New York: McGraw-Hill.

Christ, T. J. (2006). Short term estimates of growth using curriculum-based measurement of oral reading fluency: Estimates of standard error of the slope to construct confidence intervals. *School Psychology Review, 35,* 128–133.

Christ, T. J., & Ardoin, S. A. (2009). Curriculum-based measurement of oral reading: Passage equivalence and probe-set development. *Journal of School Psychology, 47,* 55–75.

Christ, T. J., & Vining, O. (2006). Curriculum-based measurement procedures to develop multiple-skill mathematics computation probes: Evaluation of random and stratified stimulus set arrangements. *School Psychology Review, 35,* 387–400.

Codding, R. S., Feinburg, A. B., Dunn, E. K., & Pace, G. M. (2005). Effects of immediate performance feedback on implementation of behavior support plans. *Journal of Applied Behavior Analysis, 38,* 205–219.

Cohen, J. (1988). *Statistical power analysis for the behavioral sciences* (2nd ed.). Hillsdale, NJ: Erlbaum.

Coie, J. D., Watt, M. F., West, S. G., Hawkins, J. D., Asarnow, J. R., Markman, H. J., et al. (1993). The science of prevention: A conceptual framework and some directions for a national research program. *American Psychologist, 48,* 1013–1022.

Coles, G. (1998). *Reading lessons: The debate over literacy.* New York: Hill and Wang.

Connell, J. E., Witt, J. C., Komatsu, C., Codding, R. & VanDerHeyden, A. M. (in submission). Recent advances in math applications curriculum-based assessments: An analysis of the relationships between applications problems, computation problems, and criterion-referenced assessments. Manuscript submitted for publication.

Cromwell, R., Blashfield, R., & Strauss, J. (1975). Criteria for classification systems. In N. Hobbs (Ed.) *Issues in the classification of children* (pp. 4–25). San Francisco: Jossey-Bass.

Cutler, U. W. (1905). *From the writings of Benjamin Franklin.* New York: Crowell.

Daly, E. J., III., Chafouleas, S., & Skinner, C. H. (2005). *Interventions for reading problems: Designing and evaluating effective strategies.* New York: Guilford.

Daly, E. J., III, Martens, B. K., Dool, E. J., & Hintze, J. M. (1998). Using brief functional analysis to select interventions for oral reading. *Journal of Behavioral Education, 8,* 203–218.

Daly, E. J., III, Martens, B. K., Hamler, K. R., Dool, E. J., & Eckert, T. L. (1999). A brief experimental analysis for identifying instructional components needed to improve oral reading fluency. *Journal of Applied Behavior Analysis, 32,* 83–94.

Daly, E. J., III, Witt, J. C., Martens, B. K., & Dool, E. J. (1997). A model for conducting a functional analysis of academic performance problems. *School Psychology Review, 26,* 554–574.

Dawes, R. M., Faust, D., & Meehl, P. E. (1989). Clinical versus actuarial judgment. *Science, 243,* 1668–1674.

Deno, S. L. (1986). Formative evaluation of individual student programs: A new role for school psychologists. *School Psychology Review, 15,* 358–374.

Deno, S. L. (2002). Problem solving as best practices. In A. Thomas & J. Grimes (Eds.), *Best practices in school psychology* (4th ed., pp. 37–56). Bethesda, MD: National Association of School Psychologists.

Deno, S. L., & Mirkin, P. K. (1977). *Data-based program modification: A manual.* Reston, VA: Council for Exceptional Children.

Donovan, M. S., & Cross, C. T. (2002). *Minority students in special and gifted education.* Washington, DC: National Academy Press.

Duhon, G. J., Mesmer, E. M., Gregerson, L., & Witt, J. C. (2009). Effects of public feedback during RtI team meetings on teacher implementation integrity and student academic performance. *Journal of School Psychology, 47,* 19–37.

Elbaum, B., Vaughn, S., Hughes, M., & Moody, S. (2000). How effective are one-to-one tutoring programs in reading for elementary students at risk for reading failure? A meta-analysis of the intervention research. *Reading Research Quarterly, 92,* 605–619.

Elliott, J., & Morrison, D. (2008). *Response to intervention blueprints for implementation: District level.* Alexandria, VA: National Association of State Directors of Special Education.

Ellis, A. K. (2005). *Research on educational innovations* (4th ed.). Larchmont, NY: Eye on Education.

Ervin, R. A., Shaughency, E., Goodman, S. D., McGlinchey, M. T., & Matthews, A. (2007). Moving from a model demonstration project to a statewide initiative in Michigan: Lessons learned from merging research-practice agendas to address reading and behavior. In S. R. Jimerson, M. K. Burns, & A. M. VanDerHeyden (Eds.), *Handbook of response to intervention: The science and practice of assessment and intervention* (pp. 354–378). New York: Springer.

Federal Register, vol. 71, no. 156, 8/14/06, p. 46647. (2006).

Feuer, M. J., Towne, L., & Shavelson, R. J. (2002). Scientific culture and educational research. *Educational Researcher, 31,* 4–14.

Foorman, B. R., Francis, D. J., & Fletcher, J. M. (1998). The role of instruction in learning to read: Preventing reading failure in at-risk children. *Journal of Educational Psychology, 90,* 37–55.

Fuchs, L. S., & Deno, S. L. (1991). Paradigmatic distinctions between instructionally relevant measurement models. *Exceptional Children*, *57*, 488–500.

Fuchs, D., Mock, D., Morgan, P. L., & Young, C. L. (2003). Responsiveness-to-intervention: Definitions, evidence, and implications for the learning disabilities construct. *Learning Disabilities Research & Practice*, *18*, 157–171.

Fuchs, L. S. (2003). Assessing intervention responsiveness: Conceptual and technical issues. *Learning Disabilities: Research & Practice*, *18*, 172–186.

Fuchs, L. S., & Fuchs, D. (1986). Effects of systematic formative evaluation: A meta-analysis. *Exceptional Children*, *53*, 199–208.

Fuchs, L. S., & Fuchs, D. (1998). Treatment validity: A unifying concept for reconceptualizing the identification of learning disabilities. *Learning Disabilities Research and Practice*, *13*, 204–219.

Fuchs, L. S., Fuchs, D., Hamlett, C. L., & Stecker, P. M. (1991). Effects of curriculum-based measurement and consultation on teacher planning and student achievement in mathematics operations. *American Educational Research Journal*, *28*, 617–641.

Fuchs, L., Fuchs, D., Hintze, J., & Lembke, E. (July, 2006). Progress monitoring in the context of responsiveness-to-intervention. Paper presented at the Summer Institute on Progress Monitoring, Kansas City, MO.

Gansle, K. A., & Noell, G. H. (2006). The fundamental role of intervention implementation in assessing resistance to intervention. In S. Jimerson, M. K. Burns, & A. M. VanDerHeyden (Eds.), *Handbook of response to intervention: The science and practice of assessment and intervention* (pp. 244–254). New York: Springer.

Gerber, M. M. (2005). Teachers are still the test: Limitations of response to instruction strategies for identifying children with learning disabilities. *Journal of Learning Disabilities*, *38*, 516–524.

Gerber, M. M., & Semmel, M. I. (1984). Teacher as imperfect test: Reconceptualizing the referral process. *Educational Psychologist*, *19*, 137–148.

Gickling, E. E. (1984, October). Operationalizing academic learning time for low achieving and handicapped mainstreamed students. Paper presented at the annual meeting of the Northern Rocky Mountain Educational Research Association, Jackson Hole, WY. (ERIC Document Reproduction Service No. ED 256 115).

Gickling, E. E., & Armstrong, D. L. (1978). Levels of instructional difficulty as related to on-task behavior, task completion, and comprehension. *Journal of Learning Disabilities*, *11*, 559–566.

Gickling, E. E., & Havertape, S. (1981). Curriculum-based assessment (CBA). Minneapolis, MN: School Psychology Inservice Training Network.

Gickling, E., & Thompson, V. (2008). A personal view of curriculum-based assessment. *Exceptional Children*, *52*, 205–218.

Gilbertson, D., Witt, J. C., Singletary, L., & VanDerHeyden, A. M. (2008). Improving teacher use of interventions: Effects of response dependent performance feedback on teacher implementation of a peer tutoring intervention. *Journal of Behavioral Education*, *16*, 311–326.

Glass, G. (1983). Effectiveness of special education. *Policy Studies Review*, *2*, 65–78.

Glover, T. A., & Albers, C. A. (2007). Considerations for evaluating universal screening assessments. *Journal of School Psychology*, *45*, 117–135.

Goals, 2000: Educate America Act of 1994. Public Law 103–227.

Good, R. H., Simmons, D. C., & Kame'enui, E. J. (2001). The importance of decision-making utility of a continuum of fluency-based indicators of foundational reading skills for third-grade high-stakes outcomes. *Scientific Studies of Reading*, *5*, 257–288.

Graden, J. L., Stollar, S. A., & Poth, R. L. (2007). The Ohio integrated systems model: Overview and lessons learned. In S. Jimerson, M. K. Burns, & A. M. VanDerHeyden (Eds.), *Handbook of response to intervention: The science and practice of assessment and intervention* (pp. 288–299). New York: Springer.

Gravois, T. A., & Gickling, E. (1997). Best practices in instructional assessment. In A. Thomas & J. Grimes (Eds.), *Best practices in school psychology*, Vol. 4 (pp. 503–518). Bethesda, MD: National Association of School Psychologists.

Greenberg, D., Ehri, L. C., & Pehrin, D. (1997). Are word-reading processes the same or different in adult literacy students and third-fifth graders matched for reading level? *Journal of Educational Psychology, 89,* 262–275.

Greenberg, M. T., Domitrovich, C., & Bumbarger, B. (1999). Preventing mental disorders in school-age children: A review of the effectiveness of prevention programs. Washington, DC: U.S. Department of Health and Human Services.

Gresham, F. M. (1991). Assessment of treatment integrity in school consultation and prereferral intervention. *School Psychology Review, 18,* 37–50.

Gresham, F. M. (2002). Responsiveness to intervention: An alternative approach to the identification of learning disabilities. In R. Bradley & L. Danielson (Eds.), *Identification of learning disabilities: Research to practice. The LEA series on special education and disability* (pp. 467–519). Mahwah, NJ: Erlbaum.

Gresham, F. M. (2007). Evolution of the response-to-intervention concept: Empirical foundations and recent developments. In S. R. Jimerson, M. K. Burns, & A. M. VanDerHeyden (Eds.), *Handbook of response to intervention: The science and practice of assessment and intervention* (pp. 10–24). New York: Springer.

Gresham, F. M., & Gansle, K. A. (1992). Misguided assumptions of DSM-III-R: Implications for school psychological practice. *School Psychology Quarterly, 7,* 79–95.

Gresham, F. M., Gansle, K. A., Noell, G. H., Cohen, S., & Rosenblum, S. (1993). Treatment integrity of school-based behavioral intervention studies: 1980–1990. *School Psychology Review, 22,* 254–272.

Gresham, F. M., MacMillan, D. L., & Bocian, K. M. (1996). Learning disabilities, low achievement, and mild mental retardation: More alike than different? *Journal of Learning Disabilities, 29,* 570–581.

Gresham, F. M., MacMillan, D. L., & Bocian, K. M. (1997). Teachers as "tests": Differential validity of teacher judgments in identifying students at-risk for learning difficulties. *School Psychology Review, 26,* 47–60.

Gresham, F. M., Reschly, D. J., Tilly, W. D., Fletcher, J., Burns, M. K., Christ, T., et al. (2005). Comprehensive evaluation of learning disabilities: A response to intervention perspective. *School Psychologist, 59,* 26–30.

Gresham, F. M., & Witt, J. C. (1997). Utility of intelligence tests for treatment planning, classification, and placement decisions: Recent empirical findings and future directions. *School Psychology Quarterly, 12,* 249–267.

Griffiths, A. J., VanDerHeyden, A. M., Skokut, M., & Lilles, E. (2009). Progress monitoring in oral reading fluency within the context of RtI. *School Psychology Quarterly, 24,* 13–23.

Hage, S. M., Romano, J. L., Conye, R. K., Kenny, M., Matthews, C., Schwartz, J. P., et al. (2007). Best practice guidelines on prevention, practice, research, training, and social advocacy for psychologists. *Journal of Counseling Psychologists, 35,* 493–566.

Hale, J. B., Naglieri, J. A., Kaufman, A. S., & Kavale, K. A. (2004, Winter). Specific learning disability classification in the new Individuals with Disabilities Education Act: The danger of good ideas. *School Psychologist, 6,* 13–29.

Hammill, D., & Larsen, S. (1974). The effectiveness of psycholinguistic training. *Exceptional Children, 41*, 5–14.

Haring, N. G., & Eaton, M. D. (1978). Systematic instructional technology: An instructional hierarchy. In N. G. Haring, T. C. Lovitt, M. D. Eaton, & C. L. Hansen (Eds.), *The fourth R: Research in the classroom* (pp. 23–40). Columbus, OH: Merrill.

Hasbrouck, J., & Tindal, G. (1987). Oral reading fluency: 90 years of measurement (Tech. Rep. No. 33). Eugene, OR: University of Oregon, College of Education, Behavioral Research and Teaching.

Hayes, S. C., Nelson, R. O., & Jarrett, R. B. (1987). The treatment utility of assessment: A functional approach to evaluating assessment quality. *American Psychologist, 42*, 963–974.

Heartland. (2004). Heartland AEA 11 annual progress report. Retrieved October 15, 2004 from http://www.aea11.k12.ia.us/downloads/2004apr.pdf.

Heartland Area Education Agency. (2002). *Program manual for special education.* Johnston, IA: Author.

Heller, K. A., Holtzman, W. H., & Messick, S. (1982). *Placing children in special education: Theories and recommendations.* Washington, DC: National Academy Press.

Hendrick Hudson School Board of Education v. Rowley. 458 U.S. 176 (1982).

Hosp, J. L. (2008). Best practices in aligning academic assessment with instruction. In A. Thomas & J. Grimes (Eds.), *Best practices in school psychology* (5th ed., pp. 363–376). Bethesda, MD: National Association of School Psychologists.

Hosp, M. K., Hosp, J. L., & Howell, K. W. (2008). *The ABCs of CBM: A practical guide to curriculum-based measurement.* New York: Guilford.

Hosp, J. L., & Reschly, D. J. (2004). Disproportionate representation of minority students in special education: Academic, demographic, and economic predictors. *Exceptional Children, 70*, 185–199.

Howell, K. W., & Nolet, V. (1999). *Curriculum-based evaluation: Teaching and decision making.* Atlanta, GA: Wadsworth.

Ikeda, M. J., & Gustafson, J. K. (2002). Heartland AEA 11's problem solving process: Impact on issues related to special education. [Research report no. 2002–01.] Johnston, IA: Heartland Area Education Agency 11.

IDEA, Individuals with Disabilities Education Improvement Act of 2004., Public Law 108-446, 108th Cong., 118 Stat. 2647 (2004) (enacted).

Iwata, B. A, Dorsey, M. F, Slifer, K. J, Bauman, K. E, & Richman, G. S. (1982). Toward a functional analysis of self-injury. *Analysis and Intervention in Developmental Disabilities, 2*, 3–20.

Jenkins, J. R., Hudson, R. F., & Johnson, E. S. (2007). Screening for at-risk readers in a response to intervention framework. *School Psychology Review, 36*, 582–600.

Jimerson, S. R., Burns, M. K., & VanDerHeyden, A. M. (2007). Response to intervention at school: The science and practice of assessment and intervention. In S. R. Jimerson, M. K. Burns, & A. M. VanDerHeyden (Eds.), *Handbook of response to intervention: The science and practice of assessment and intervention* (pp. 3–9). New York: Springer.

Johnson v. Upland, 26 Fed. Appx. 689, 2002 U.S. App. LEXUS 515 (9th Cir. 2002).

Jones, K. M., & Wickstrom, K. F. (2002). Done in sixty seconds: Further analysis of the brief assessment model for academic problems. *School Psychology Review, 31*, 554–568.

Joseph, L. M. (2000). Developing first graders' phonemic awareness, word identification, and spelling: A comparison of two contemporary phonic instructional approaches. *Reading Research and Instruction, 39*, 160–169.

Kamii, C., & Manning, M. (2005). Dynamic indicators of basic early literacy skills: A tool for evaluating student learning. *Journal of Research in Childhood Education, 20*, 75–90.

Kaminski, R. A., & Good, R. H. (1999). Assessing early literacy skills in a problem-solving model: Dynamic indicators of basic early literacy skills. In M. R. Shinn (Ed.) *Advanced applications of curriculum-based measurement* (pp. 113–142). New York: Guilford.

Kavale, K. A., & Forness, S. R. (1999). Effectiveness of special education. In C. R. Reynolds & T. B. Gutkin (Eds.), *The handbook of school psychology* (3rd ed., pp. 984–1024). New York: Wiley.

Kavale, K. A., & Forness, S. R. (2000). Policy decisions in special education: The role of meta-analysis. In R. Gersten, E. P. Schiller, & S. Vaughn (Eds.), *Contemporary special education research: Synthesis of the knowledge base on critical instructional issues* (pp. 281–326). Mahway, NJ: Erlbaum.

Kazdin, A. E. (1982). *Single-case research designs: Methods for clinical and applied settings.* New York: Oxford.

Kirk, S. A., McCarthy, J., & Kirk, W. D. (1961). The Illinois test of psycholinguistic abilities. Urbana, IL: University of Illinois Press.

Kovaleski, J. F., Gickling, E. E., Morrow, H., & Swank, P. R. (1998). High versus low implementation of instructional support teams: A case for maintaining program fidelity. *Remedial and Special Education, 20*, 170–183.

Kovaleski, J. F., Tucker, J. A., & Duffy, D. J. (1995). School reform through instructional support: The Pennsylvania Initiative (Part I). *Communiqué, 23*(8) (insert).

Kovaleski, J. F., Tucker, J. A., & Stevens, L. J. (1996). Bridging special and regular education: The Pennsylvania Initiative. *Educational Leadership, 53*, 44–47.

Kurns, S., & Tilly, W. D. (2008). *Response to intervention blueprints for implementation: School building level.* Alexandria, VA: National Association of State Directors of Special Education.

Kysar, K. (2008). Voices from the field—Central Elementary: Yukon, Oklahoma. Retrieved from http://www.rtinetwork.org/Connect/Voices/Central-Elementary-School-Yukon-Oklahoma, July 22, 2009.

Lau, M. Y., Sieler, J. D., Muyskens, P., Canter, A., Vankeuren, B., & Marston, D. (2006). Perspectives on the use of the problem-solving model from the viewpoint of a school psychologist, administrator, and teacher from a large Midwest urban school district. *Psychology in the Schools, 43*, 117–127.

Lennon, J. E., & Slesinski, C. (1999). Early intervention in reading: Results of a screening and intervention program for kindergarten students. *School Psychology Review, 28*, 353–364.

Lentz, F. E., & Shapiro, E. S. (1986). Functional assessment of the academic environment. *School Psychology Review, 15*, 346–357.

Levine, D. U., & Lezotte, L. W. (1990). *Unusually effective schools: A review and analysis of research and practice.* Madison, WI: National Centre for Effective Schools Research and Development.

Losardo, A., & Bricker, D. (1994). Activity-based intervention and direct instruction: A comparison study. *American Journal on Mental Retardation, 98*, 744–765.

Lovett, M. W., Borden, S. L., Lacerenza, L., Benson, N. J., & Brackstone, D. (1994). Treating the core deficits of developmental dyslexia: Evidence of transfer of learning after phonologically- and strategy-based reading training programs. *Journal of Educational Psychology, 30*, 805–822.

Lyon, G. R. (1995). Toward a definition of dyslexia. *Annals of Dyslexia, 45*, 3–27.

Mace, F. C., Yankanich, M. A., & West, B. J. (1988). Toward a methodology of experimental analysis and treatment of aberrant classroom behaviors. *Special Services in the Schools, 4*, 71–88.

MacMillan, D. L. (1998). Unpackaging special education categorical variables in the study and teaching of children with conduct problems. *Education and Treatment of Children, 21*, 234–245.

MacMillan, D. L., Gresham, F. M., & Bocian, K. M. (1998). Discrepancy between definitions of learning disabilities and school practices: An empirical investigation. *Journal of Learning Disabilities, 31,* 314–326.

MacMillan, D. L., & Speece, D. L. (1999). Utility of current diagnostic categories for research and practice. In R. Gallimore & L. P. Bernheimer (Eds.), *Developmental perspectives on children with high-incidence disabilities, The LEA series on special education and disability* (pp. 111–133). Mahwah, NJ: Erlbaum.

Mann, L. (1971). Psychometric phrenology and the new faculty psychology: The case against ability assessment and training. *Journal of Special Education, 5,* 3–14.

Manzo, K. K., & Galley, M. (2003). Math climbs, reading flat on '03 NAEP. *Education Week, 23,* 1–18.

Marston, D., Mirkin, P., & Deno, S. (1984). Curriculum-based measurement: An alternative to traditional screening, referral, and identification. *Journal of Special Education, 18,* 109–117.

Marston, D., Muyskens, P., Lau, M., & Canter, A. (2003). Problem-solving model for decision making with high-incidence disabilities: The Minneapolis experience. *Learning Disabilities Research & Practice, 18,* 187–200.

McComas, J. J., Hoch, H., & Mace, F. C. (2000). Functional analysis. In E. S. Shapiro & T. R. Kratochwill (Eds.), *Conducting school-based assessments of child and adolescent behavior* (pp. 78–120). New York: Guilford.

McComas, J. J., & Mace, F. C. (2000). Theory and practice in conducting functional analysis. In E. S. Shapiro, & T. R. Kratochwill (Eds.), *Behavioral assessment in schools: Theory, research, and clinical foundations* (2nd ed., pp. 78–103). New York: Guilford.

McGee, S. (2001). *Evidence-based physical diagnosis.* Philadelphia: Harcourt.

McGuinness, C., McGuinness, D., & McGuinness, G. (1996). Phono-graphix: A new method for remediating reading difficulties. *Annals of Dyslexia, 46,* 73–96.

McMaster, K. L., Fuchs, D., Fuchs, L. S., & Compton, D. L. (2005). Responding to nonresponders: An experimental field trial of identification and intervention methods. *Exceptional Children, 71,* 445–463.

McNamara, K., & Hollinger, C. (2003). Intervention-based assessment: Evaluation rates and eligibility findings. *Exceptional Children, 69,* 181–194.

Meehl, P. E., & Rosen, A. (1955). Antecedent probability and the efficiency of psychometric signs, patterns, or cutting scores. *Psychological Bulletin, 52,* 194–215.

Messick, S. (1995). Validity of psychological assessment: Validation of inferences from persons' responses and performances as scientific inquiry into score meaning. *American Psychologist, 50,* 741–749.

Minneapolis Public Schools. (2001). *Problem solving model: Introduction for all staff.* Minneapolis, MN: Author.

Mirkin, P., Deno, S., Tindal, G., & Kuehnle, K. (1982). Frequency of measurement and data utilization as factors in standardized behavioral assessment of academic skill. *Journal of Psychopathology and Behavioral Assessment, 4,* 361–370.

Mortenson, B. P., & Witt, J. C. (1998). The use of weekly performance feedback to increase teacher implementation of a prereferral academic intervention. *School Psychology Review, 27,* 613–627.

National Association of School Psychologists. (2000). *Professional conduct manual.* Bethesda, MD: Author.

National Center for Educational Statistics. (2005). *The nation's report card (NAEP).* Washington, DC: Author.

National Center on Response to Intervention. (2009). *RtI.* Accessed January 18, 2010, from www.rti4success.org

National Reading Panel (2000). *Report of the National Reading Panel: Teaching children to read.* Washington, D.C.: U.S. Department of Health and Human Services.

NCLB, No Child Left Behind Act of 2001. Public Law 107–110, 107th Cong., 115 Stat. 1425. (2002). (enacted).

Noell, G. H., Duhon, G. J., Gatti, S. L., & Connell, J. E. (2002). Consultation, follow-up, and implementation of behavior management interventions in general education. *School Psychology Review, 31,* 217–234.

Noell, G. H., & Gansle, K. A. (2006). Assuring the form has substance: Treatment plan implementation as the foundation of assessing response to intervention. *Assessment for Effective Intervention, 32,* 32–39.

Noell, G. H., Gansle, K. A., Witt, J. C., Whitmarsh, E. L., Freeland, J. T., LaFleur, L. H., et al. (1998). Effects of contingent reward and instruction on oral reading performance at differing levels of passage difficulty. *Journal of Applied Behavior Analysis, 31,* 659–663.

Noell, G. H., Witt, J. C., Gilbertson, D. N., Ranier, D. D., & Freeland, J. T. (1997). Increasing teacher intervention implementation in general education settings through consultation and performance feedback. *School Psychology Quarterly, 12,* 77–88.

Noell, G. H., Witt, J. C., LaFleur, L. H., Mortenson, B. P., Ranier, D. D., & LeVelle, J. (2000). A comparison of two follow-up strategies to increase teacher intervention implementation in general education following consultation. *Journal of Applied Behavior Analysis, 33,* 271–284.

Noell, G. H., Witt, J. C., Slider, N. J., Connell, J. E., Gatti, S. L., Williams, K. L., et al. (2005). Treatment implementation following behavioral consultation in schools: A comparison of three follow-up strategies. *School Psychology Review, 34,* 87–106.

Northwest Evaluation Association. (2003). *Measures of academic progress.* Lake Oswego, OR: Author.

Nussbaum, S. (2006). Prevention: The cornerstone of quality health care. *American Journal of Preventive Medicine, 31,* 107–108.

O'Connor, R. E., Fulmer, D., Harty, K. R., & Bell, K. M. (2005). Layers of reading intervention in kindergarten through third grade: Changes in teaching and student outcomes. *Journal of Learning Disabilities, 38,* 440–455.

O'Connor, R. E., White, A., & Swanson, H. L. (2007). Repeated reading versus continuous reading: Influences on reading fluency and comprehension. *Exceptional Children, 74,* 31–46.

Odom, S. L., Brantlinger, E., Gersten, R., Horner, R. H., Thompson, B., & Harris, K. R. (2005). Research in special education: Scientific methods and evidence-based practices. *Exceptional Children, 71,* 137–148.

Olson, S. C., Daly, E. J., Andersen, M., Turner, A., & LeClair, C. (2007). Assessing student response to intervention. In S. R. Jimerson, M. K. Burns, & A. M. VanDerHeyden (Eds.), *Handbook of response to intervention: The science and practice of assessment and intervention* (pp. 117–129). New York: Springer.

Petursdottir, A. L., McMaster, K., McComas, J. J., Bradfield, T., Braganza, V., Koch-Mcdonald, J., et al. (2009). Brief experimental analysis of early reading interventions. *Journal of School Psychology, 47,* 215–243.

Renaissance Learning. (1998). *STAR math.* Wisconsin Rapids, WI: Author.

Renaissance Learning. (2003). *STAR reading.* Wisconsin Rapids, WI: Author.

Reschly, A. L., Coolong-Chaffin, M., Christenson, S. L., & Gutkin, T. (2007). Contextual influences and response to intervention: Critical issues and strategies. In S. R. Jimerson, M. K. Burns, & A. M. VanDerHeyden (Eds.), *Handbook of response to intervention: The science and practice of assessment and intervention* (pp. 148–160). New York: Springer.

Reschly, D. J. (1996). Functional assessments and special education decision making. In W. Stainback & S. Stainback (Eds.), *Controversial issues confronting special education: Divergent perspectives* (2nd ed., pp. 115–128). Boston: Allyn and Bacon.

Reschly, D. J., & Starkweather, A. R. (1997). *Evaluation of an alternative special education assessment and classification program in the Minneapolis Public Schools*. Minneapolis, MN: Minneapolis Public Schools.

Reynolds, M. C. (1975). Trends in special education: Implications for measurement. In W. Hively & M. C. Reynolds (Eds.), *Domain-referenced testing in special education* (pp. 15–28). Minneapolis: University of Minnesota Leadership Training Institute/Special Education.

Reynolds, M. C. (1991). Classification and labeling. In J. W. Lloyd, A. C. Repp, & N. N. Singh (Eds.), *The regular education initiative: Alternative perspectives on concepts, issues, and models* (pp. 407–419). Sycamore, IL: Sycamore.

Reynolds, C. R., & Shaywitz, S. E. (2009a). Ready or not? Or, from wait-to-fail to watch-them-fail. *School Psychology Quarterly, 24*, 130–145.

Reynolds, C. R., & Shaywitz, S. E. (2009b). Response to intervention: Prevention and remediation, perhaps. Diagnosis no. *Child Developmental Perspectives, 3*, 44–47.

Riley-Tillman, T. C., & Burns, M. K. (2009). *Single case design for measuring response to educational intervention*. New York: Guilford.

Roehrig, A., Petscher, Y., Nettles, S. M., Hudson, R. F., & Torgesen, J. K. (2008). Accuracy of the DIBELS oral reading fluency measure for predicting third-grade reading comprehension outcomes. *Journal of School Psychology, 46*, 343–366.

Rothstein, R., & Jacobsen, R. (2006). The goals of education. *Phi Delta Kappan, 88*, 264–272.

Salvia, J., Ysseldyke, J. E., & Bolt, S. E. (2009). *Assessment in special and inclusive education* (11th ed.). Boston: Houghton Mifflin.

Sanetti, L. M., & Kratochwill, T. R. (2009). Treatment integrity assessment in the schools: An evaluation of the Treatment Integrity Planning Protocol (TIPP). *School Psychology Quarterly, 24*, 24–35.

Sarason, S. (1996). *Revisiting the culture of school and the problem of change*. New York: Teachers College Press.

Schatschneider, C., Wagner, R. K., & Crawford, E. C. (2009). The importance of measuring growth in response to intervention models: Testing a core assumption. *Learning and Individual Differences, 18*, 308–315.

Schulte, A. C. (2008). Measurement in school consultation research. In W. P. Erchul & S. M. Sheridan (Eds.), *Handbook of research in school consultation* (pp. 33–61). New York: Erlbaum.

Scruggs, T. E., & Mastropieri, M. A. (2002). On babies and bathwater: Addressing the problems of identification of learning disabilities. *Learning Disability Quarterly, 25*, 155–168.

Shapiro, E. S. (2004). *Academic skill problems: Direct assessment and intervention* (3rd ed.) New York: Guilford.

Shapiro, E. S. (2009, March). *How are progress monitoring data used in the evaluation of RtI?* Paper presented at the Southeastern Regional Conference on Response to Intervention, Washington, DC.

Shapiro, E. S., & Clemens, N. H. (in press). A conceptual model for evaluating system effects of response to intervention. *Assessment for Effective Intervention*.

Shinn, M. R. (Ed.) (1989). *Curriculum-based measurement: Assessing special children*. New York: Guilford.

Shinn, M. R., Tindal, G. A., & Spira, D. A. (1987). Special education referrals as an index of teacher tolerance: Are teachers imperfect tests? *Exceptional Children, 54*, 32–40.

Silberglitt, B., & Gibbons, K. A. (2005). *Establishing slope targets for use in a response to intervention model* (Technical Manual). Rush City, MN: St. Croix River Education District.

Simos, P. G., Fletcher, J. M., Bergman, E., Breier, J. I., Foorman, B. R., Castillo, E. M., et al. (2001). Dyslexia-specific brain activation profile becomes normal following successful remedial training. *Neurology, 58*, 1203–1213.

Siegel, L. S. (1988). Evidence that IQ scores are irrelevant to the definition and analysis of reading disability. *Canadian Journal of Psychology, 42*, 201–215.

Siegel, L. S. (1993). Phonological processing deficits as the basis of a reading disability. *Developmental Review Special Issue: Phonological Processes and Learning Disability, 13*, 246–257.

Slavin, R. E., & Lake, C. (2008). Effective programs in elementary mathematics: A best-evidence synthesis. *Review of Educational Research, 78*, 427–515.

Snow, C. E., Burns, M. S., & Griffin, P. (1998). *Preventing reading difficulties in young children.* Washington, DC: National Research Council.

Sornson, R., Frost, F., & Burns, M. K. (2005). Instructional support teams in Michigan: Data from Northville Public Schools. *Communiqué, 33*, 28–30.

Speece, D. L. (2005). Hitting the moving target known as reading development: Some thoughts on screening children for secondary interventions. *Journal of Learning Disabilities, 38*, 487–493.

Speece, D. L., & Case, L. P. (2001). Classification in context: An alternative approach to identifying early reading disability. *Journal of Educational Psychology, 93*, 735–749.

Speece, D. L., Case, L. P., & Molloy, D. E. (2003). Responsiveness to general education instruction as the first gate to learning disabilities identification. *Learning Disabilities Research and Practice, 18*, 147–156.

Stanovich, K. E., & Siegel, L. S. (1994). Phenotypic performance profile of children with reading disabilities: A regression-based test of the phonological-core variable-difference model. *Journal of Educational Psychology, 86*, 24–53.

Starlin, C. M., & Starlin, A. (1973). *Guides to decision making in oral reading.* Bemidji, MN: Unique Curriculums.

Stewart, L. H., & Silberglitt, B. (2005). Best practices in developing academic local norms. In A. Thomas & J. Grimes (Eds.), *Best practices in school psychology* (5th ed., pp. 225–242). Bethesda, MD: National Association of School Psychologists.

Stiggins, R. (2005). From formative assessment to assessment FOR learning: A path to success in standards-based schools. *Phi Delta Kappan, 87*, 324–328.

Stith, S., Pruitt, I., Dees, J., Fronce, M., Green, N., Som, A., et al. (2006). Implementing community-based prevention programming: A review of the literature. *Journal of Primary Prevention, 27*, 599–617.

Stuebing, K., Fletcher, J., LeDoux, J., Lyon, G. R., Shaywitz, S., & Shaywitz, B. (2002). Validity of IQ-discrepancy classifications of reading disabilities: A meta-analysis. *American Educational Research Journal, 39*, 469–518.

Sugai, G., & Horner, R. (2006) A promising approach for expanding and sustaining the implementation of school-wide positive behavior support. *School Psychology Review, 35*, 245–259.

Swanson, H. L. (1999). Instructional components that predict treatment outcomes for students with learning disabilities: Support for a combined strategy and direct instruction model. *Learning Disabilities Research & Practice, 14*, 129–140.

Swanson, H. L. (2000). What instruction works for students with learning disabilities? Summarizing the results from a meta-analysis of intervention studies. In R. M. Gersten, E. P. Schiller, & S. Vaughn (Eds.), *Contemporary special education research: Syntheses of the knowledge base on critical instructional issues* (pp. 1–30). Mahwah, NJ: Erlbaum.

Swanson, H. L., Hoskyn, M., & Lee, C. (1999). *Interventions for students with learning disabilities: A meta-analysis of treatment outcomes.* New York: Guilford Press.

Telzrow, C. F., McNamara, K., & Hollinger, C. L. (2000). Fidelity of problem-solving implementation and relationship to student performance. *School Psychology Review, 29*, 443–461.

Tilly, W. D., III (2002). Best practices in school psychology as a problem-solving enterprise. In A. Thomas & J. Grimes (Eds.), *Best practices in school psychology* (4th ed., pp. 21–36). Bethesda, MD: National Association of School Psychologists.

Tilly, W. D., III (2003). *How many tiers are needed for successful prevention and early intervention? Heartland Area Education Agency's evolution from four to three tiers.* Paper presented at the National Research Center on Learning Disabilities Responsiveness-to-Intervention Symposium, Kansas City, MO.

Tilly, W. D., III (2008). The evolution of school psychology to science-based practice: Problem solving and the three-tiered model. In A. Thomas & J. Grimes (Eds.), *Best practices in school psychology* (5th ed., pp. 17–36). Bethesda, MD: National Association of School Psychology.

Torgesen, J. K., Alexander, A. W., Wagner, R. K., Rashotte, C. A., Voeller, K. K. S., & Conway, T. (2001). Intensive remedial instruction for children with severe reading disabilities: Immediate and long-term outcomes from two instructional approaches. *Journal of Learning Disabilities, 34*, 33–58.

Torgesen, J. K., Rose, E., Lindamood, P., Conway, T, & Garvan, C. (1999). Preventing reading failure in young children with phonological processing disabilities: Group and individual responses to instruction. *Journal of Educational Psychology, 91*, 579–594.

Treptow, M. A., Burns, M. K., & McComas, J. J. (2006). Reading at the frustration, instructional, and independent levels: Effects on student time on task and comprehension. *School Psychology Review, 36*, 159–166.

Tucker, J. A. (1989). *Basic flashcard technique when vocabulary is the goal.* Unpublished teaching materials. University of Tennessee at Chattanooga. Chattanooga, TN: Author.

Tucker, J. A. (2001). Instructional support teams: It's a group thing. In B. Sornson (Ed.) *Preventing early learning failure* (pp. 47–63). Alexandria, VA: Association for Supervision & Curriculum Development.

U.S. Department of Education, National Assessment of Educational Progress. (2002). *Writing assessment and unpublished tabulations.* Washington, DC: National Center for Educational Statistics.

U.S. Department of Education, Office of Special Education and Rehabilitative Services, Office of Special Education Programs. (2006). 28th Annual Report to Congress on the Implementation of the Individuals with Disabilities Education Act. Washington, DC: Author.

VanDerHeyden, A. M. (2005). Intervention-driven assessment practices in early childhood/early intervention: Measuring what is possible instead of what is present. *Journal of Early Intervention, 28*, 28–33.

VanDerHeyden, A. M., & Burns, M. K. (2005). Using curriculum-based assessment and curriculum-based measurement to guide elementary mathematics instruction: Effect on individual and group accountability scores. *Assessment for Effective Intervention, 30*, 15–29.

VanDerHeyden, A. M., Snyder, P., Broussard, C., & Ramsdell, K. (2008). Measuring response to early literacy intervention with preschoolers at risk. *Topics in Early Childhood Special Education, 27*, 232–249.

VanDerHeyden, A. M., & Witt, J. C. (2005). Quantifying the context of assessment: Capturing the effect of base rates on teacher referral and a problem-solving model of identification. *School Psychology Review, 34*, 161–183.

VanDerHeyden, A. M., & Witt, J. C. (2008). Selecting and implementing interventions. What do I do when . . . In *The answer book on RtI* (chap. 5). Palm Beach Gardens, FL: LRP Publications.

VanDerHeyden, A. M., Witt, J. C., & Barnett, D. A. (2005). The emergence and possible futures of response to intervention. *Journal of Psychoeducational Assessment, 23*, 339–361.

VanDerHeyden, A. M., Witt, J. C., & Gilbertson, D. A. (2007). Multi-year evaluation of the effects of a response to intervention (RtI) model on identification of children for special education. *Journal of School Psychology, 45,* 225–256.

VanDerHeyden, A. M., Witt, J. C., & Naquin, G. (2003). Development and validation of a process for screening referrals to special education. *School Psychology Review, 32,* 204–227.

Vaughn, S., Cirino, P. T., Wanzek, J., Wexler, J., Fletcher, J. M., Denton, C. D., et al. (in press). Response to intervention for middle school students with reading difficulties: Effects of a primary and secondary intervention. *School Psychology Review.*

Vaughn, S., Gersten, R., & Chard, D. J. (2000). The underlying message in LD intervention research: Findings from research syntheses. *Exceptional Children, 67,* 99–114.

Vaughn, S., Linan-Thompson, S., & Hickman, P. (2003). Response to instruction as a means of identifying students with reading/learning disabilities. *Exceptional Children, 69,* 391–409.

Vaughn, S., Wanzek, J., Linan-Thompson, S., & Murray, C. (2007). Monitoring response to intervention for students at-risk for reading difficulties: High and low responders. In S. R. Jimerson, M. K. Burns, & A. M. VanDerHeyden (Eds.), *The handbook of response to intervention: The science and practice of assessment and intervention,* (pp 234–243). New York: Springer.

Vellutino, F. R., Scanlon, D. M., & Lyon, G. R. (2000). Differentiating between difficult-to-remediate and readily remediated poor readers: More evidence against the IQ-achievement discrepancy definition of reading disability. *Journal of Learning Disabilities, 33,* 223–238.

Vellutino, F., Scanlon, D., Sipay, E., Small, S., Pratt, A., Chen, R., et al. (1996). Cognitive profiles of difficult-to-remediate and readily remediated poor readers: Early intervention as a vehicle for distinguishing between cognitive and experiential deficits as basic causes of specific reading disability. *Journal of Educational Psychology, 88,* 601–638.

Vellutino, F. R., Scanlon, D. M., & Tanzman, M. S. (1998). The case for early intervention in diagnosing specific reading disability. *Journal of School Psychology, 36,* 367–397.

Wackerle, A. K., Boice, C. H., Christ, T. J., & Burns, M. K. (2006). Response to intervention at NASP: Were 44 presentations enough? *Communiqué, 34,* 20–21.

Wagner, D., McComas, J. J., Bollman, K., & Holton, E. (2006). The use of functional reading analysis to identify effective reading interventions. *Assessment for Effective Intervention, 32,* 40–49.

Weissler, A. M. (1999). A perspective on standardizing the predictive power of noninvasive cardiovascular tests by likelihood ratio computation: Mathematical principles. *Mayo Clinic Procedures, 74,* 1061–1071.

Wickstrom, K. F., Jones, K. M., LaFleur, L. H., & Witt, J. C. (1998). An analysis of treatment integrity in school-based behavioral consultation. *School Psychology Quarterly, 13,* 141–154.

Wilson, D. B., Gottfredson, D. C., & Najaka, S. S. (2001). School-based prevention of problem behaviors: A meta-analysis. *Journal for Quantitative Criminology, 17,* 247–272.

Windram, H., Scierka, B., & Silberglitt, B. (2007). Response to intervention at the secondary level: Two districts' models of implementation. *Communiqué, 35,* 43–45.

Wise, B. W., Ring, J., & Olson, R. K. (1999). Training phonological awareness with and without explicit attention to articulation. *Journal of Experimental Child Psychology, 72,* 271–304.

Witt, J. C., Noell, G. H., LaFleur, L. H., & Mortenson, B. P. (1997). Teacher use of interventions in general education settings: Measurement and analysis of the independent variable. *Journal of Applied Behavior Analysis, 30,* 693–696.

Ysseldyke, J. E. (2005). Assessment and decision making for students with learning disabilities: What if this is as good as it gets? *Learning Disability Quarterly, 28,* 125–128.

Ysseldyke, J. E., Algozzine, B., & Epps, S. (1983). A logical and empirical analysis of current practice in classifying students as handicapped. *Exceptional Children, 50,* 160–166.

Ysseldyke, J. E., & Marston, D. (2000). Origins of categorical special education services in schools and a rationale for changing them. In D. Reschly, D. Tilley, & J. Grimes (Eds.), *Functional and noncategorical special education* (pp. 137–146). Longmont, CO: Sopris West.

Ysseldyke, J. E., O'Sullivan, P. J., Thurlow, M. L., & Christenson, S. L. (1989). Qualitative differences in reading and math instruction received by handicapped students. *Remedial and Special Education, 10*, 14–20.

Ysseldyke, J. E., & Salvia, J. (1974). Diagnostic-prescriptive teaching: Two models. *Exceptional Children, 41*, 181–186.

Ysseldyke, J. E., Vanderwood, M. L., & Shriner, J. (1997). Changes over the past decade in special education referral to placement probability: An incredibly reliable practice. *Diagnostique, 23*, 193–201.

Annotated Bibliography

Barnett, D. W., Daly, E. J., III, Jones, K. M., & Lentz, F. E., Jr. (2004). Response to intervention: Empirically-based special service decisions from increasing and decreasing intensity single case designs. *Journal of Special Education*, 38, 66–79.

This paper provides a model for using single-case research designs (SCD) within an RtI framework. An effective SCD for RtI should include a meaningful outcome variable that can be measured frequently across time and includes interventions with increasing and measureable intensity. Interventions are considered more intensive if they require more adult supervision or an increased amount of modifications to the curriculum. Designs can begin with low intensity and increase or with high intensity and decrease over time as needed.

Burns, M. K., & Gibbons, K. (2008). Response to intervention implementation in elementary and secondary schools: Procedures to assure scientific-based practices. New York: Routledge.

This book includes implementation guidelines for RtI at both the elementary and secondary levels. In addition, it includes a CD that contains various forms and problem-solving checklists.

Burns, M., Appleton, J. J., & Stehouwer, J. D. (2005). Meta-analytic review of responsiveness-to-intervention research: Examining field-based and research-implemented models. *Journal of Psychoeducational Assessment*, 23, 381–394.

This meta-analysis synthesized research studies. Studies were categorized as large-scale models already in practice or models implemented for research. Both types of models had strong effects on student (e.g., academic skill assessments, time on task, and growth on a particular skill) and system (e.g., reductions in referrals to and placements into special education) outcomes. The field-based models tended to have stronger effects for systematic outcomes than the research-implemented models. Moreover, less than 2% of students were identified as SLD among studies reviewing large-scale models.

Case, L. P., Speece, D. L., & Molloy, D. E. (2003). The validity of a response-to-instruction paradigm to identify reading disabilities: A longitudinal analysis of individual differences and contextual factors. *School Psychology Review*, 32, 557–582.

This study implemented the treatment validity model articulated by Fuchs and Fuchs (1998) in which: (a) the overall rate of student response in the classroom is assessed to determine if the instructional environment is adequate; (b) students are then identified as needing additional remediation from a sound instructional environment when the student's level and slope of growth are below the student's peers (dually discrepant; DD); and (c) assessment results are used to enhance instruction and develop appropriate interventions in the general education setting.

The study occurred in one elementary school that served 680 students. Students were identified as at risk if their scores fell below the 25th percentile in their respective classrooms. The results indicated that the RtI model discussed in this study allowed for accurate identification of students in need of more intensive services (i.e., special education).

Foorman, B. R., Francis, D. J., & Fletcher, J. M. (1998). The role of instruction in learning to read: Preventing reading failure in at-risk children. *Journal of Educational Psychology, 90,* 37–55.

This seminal study compared three instructional strategies (i.e., direct, embedded, or implicit) to determine which led to the greatest and most rapid student gains in reading. Data were collected from 285 first- and second-grade students at risk for reading failure. Direct instruction involved explicit instruction of decoding phonemes in decodable text; embedded instruction taught decoding phonemes by providing instruction on sound-spelling relationships in connected text by embedding the association within more naturalistic tasks; and implicit instruction relied on connected text without explicit instruction in how to decode phonemes. Students in the direct instruction condition increased their word-reading skills significantly more rapidly than children taught with the other two strategies. Although 16% of the students who received direct instruction failed to demonstrate reading growth, 44% of the students who received embedded instruction and 46% of those in the implicit instruction condition did not demonstrate reading growth.

Fuchs, L. S. (2003). Assessing intervention responsiveness: Conceptual and technical issues. *Learning Disabilities: Research & Practice, 18,* 172–186.

This article reviews research regarding the assessment of student response to intervention. Although this paper did not coin the term "dual discrepancy," it did provide one of the clearest descriptions of it. The author describes three approaches for measuring adequate response:

1. *Final status.* Students are measured at the end of the intervention.
2. *Growth model.* Students are monitored periodically throughout the intervention, and decisions are made on amount of learning, not considering if students reached a level of performance.
3. *Dual discrepancy.* This method measures both performance level and growth rate.

There are several criteria with which final status and growth models can be evaluated, including (a) normative (compare to all students in the distribution, e.g., below the 25th percentile); (b) limited norm (the group is limited to a subset of students in the school); and (c) benchmark (a standard that has been correlated to successful outcomes, such as scoring proficiently on state reading tests). Previous research indicated that measuring student response to intervention can improve consequential and construct validity of identification decisions.

Griffiths, A. J., Parson, L. B., Burns, M. K., VanDerHeyden, A. M., & Tilly, W. D. *Response to intervention: Research for practice.* Alexandria, VA: National Association of State Directors of Special Education.

This annotated bibliography summarizes research findings that underpin RtI assessment, implementation, and decision making. Accessed for free at http://www.nasdse.org/Portals/0/Documents/Download%20Publications/PNA-0776.pdf.

Jimerson, S. R., Burns, M. K., & VanDerHeyden, A. M. (Eds). (2007). *Handbook of response to intervention: The science and practice of assessment and intervention.* New York: Springer.

This book is a go-to reference summarizing the research base from which RtI practices have evolved.

Marston, D., Muyskens, P., Lau, M., & Canter, A. (2003). Problem-solving model for decision making with high-incidence disabilities: The Minneapolis experience. *Learning Disabilities Research & Practice, 18,* 187–200.

This paper described the Minneapolis Public Schools' problem-solving model (PSM) as a three-stage model that evaluates an individual student's academic needs, plans interventions, and measures response to intervention to make special education eligibility decisions. Data provided here found that although the number of special education placements did not decline outcomes improved. Moreover, roles changed for school personnel including teachers, special education teachers, and school psychologists.

Peacock, G. G., Ervin, R. A., Daly, E. J., & Merrell, K. W. (Eds). (2009). *Practical handbook of school psychology: Effective practices for the 21st century.* New York: Guilford.

This book provides practical guidance for those who wish to use data to identify learning problems, develop interventions, and monitor intervention effects in schools.

Shapiro, E. S. (2004). *Academic skills problems* (3rd ed.) *Direct assessment and intervention.* New York: Guilford.

This book provides a framework for assessing and resolving academic performance problems in schools.

Shinn, M. R. (Ed.). (1989). *Curriculum-based measurement: Assessing special children.* New York: Guilford.

This book provides a summary of the early research on curriculum-based measurement and describes how CBM data can be used to inform instructional decisions.

Shinn, M. R. (Ed.). (1998). Advanced applications of curriculum-based measurement. New York: Guilford.

This book describes the evolution of curriculum-based measurement to address system learning problems and to assess the performance of students from more diverse backgrounds (e.g., ethnicity, primary language, and age).

Stuebing, K., Fletcher, J., LeDoux, J., Lyon, G. R., Shaywitz, S., & Shaywitz, B. (2002). Validity of IQ-discrepancy classifications of reading disabilities: A meta-analysis. *American Educational Research Journal,* 39, 469–518.

This influential meta-analysis examined 46 studies that addressed the validity of the IQ-achievement discrepancy as a classification for low-performing readers. The IQ-discrepant and IQ-consistent groups did not differ in academic performance and differed only slightly in cognitive ability. Moreover, low-performing readers with and without discrepancies did not differ in phonological awareness, rapid naming, verbal short-term memory, and vocabulary skills. Thus, these data provide a substantial amount of evidence against the IQ-achievement discrepancy model as a valid criterion for SLD.

VanDerHeyden, A. M., Witt, J. C., & Gilbertson, D. (2007). Multi-year evaluation of the effects of a response to intervention model on identification of children for special education. *Journal of School Psychology,* 45, 225–256.

This study investigated the effect of an RtI model on district-wide special education evaluation and eligibility determinations. The STEEP RtI model was implemented in five elementary schools, with two schools in the first year, a third school in the second year, and two schools in the final year. The research design included a reversal at one of the schools to examine the effect of removal and then reinstatement of the RtI model. The intervention relied on "can't do/won't do" assessments, survey assessments, and a standard-protocol intervention for approximately 10 minutes a day for 10 to 15 days. The number of special education evaluations decreased by 40% to 70% after implementation, and the number of children identified as SLD in the district decreased from 6% to 3.5% in 1 year. Across three schools, the school-based team used the RtI data to make decisions about student eligibility approximately 62% of the time in the first year. In most cases where the teams did not follow the RtI data, an adequate RtI had occurred but the team decided to refer for evaluation anyway. Team decisions corresponded to the RtI data much more frequently (better than 90%) in year 2.

Index

Specificity, 44–47, 67, 106
St. Croix River Education District
(Minnesota), 13
Standard protocol interventions,
31, 32
Star Math, 8
Star Reading, 8
State accountability tests, 70–73
State performance standards, 20
STEEP, 13, 93
Student learning
as focus of RtI, 100, 108, 109, 111
outcomes, recommendations for
evaluating, 66
Tier 2 intervention, 32, 33, 66
Student need, interventions based on
as component of RtI, 6
Successive hurdles approach, 47
System level problems, 23, 63, 66,
107, 108. *See also* Class-wide
learning problems; Grade-wide
problems
System to Enhance Educational
Performance. *See* Screening to
Enhance Educational Progress
(STEEP)

T
Task difficulty, 58, 59, 64
Teacher identification as screening
tool, 19, 35, 105, 106
Teacher referral, 19, 35, 36, 38, 42, 105,
106
Teachers
attitudes toward RtI, 101
and class-wide intervention, 26.
See also Class-wide interventions

and class-wide learning problems,
26. *See also* Class-wide learning
problems
grade-level teams, 24
impact of RtI on, 91, 92
and intervention implementation,
32, 64, 65
professional development, 26, 31,
102
and progress monitoring,
importance of, 80
role of in early implementation
models, 12, 13
and screening task selection, 20, 24
special education, 109, 110
Technical adequacy of RtI
classification agreements, 43–47
classification analyses, 37, 40, 41
conditional probabilities, 41–43
data-based decision making, 61
and decision making, 38, 39
decision rules or cut points,
derivation of, 48–50. *See also*
Decision rules and cut points
dependent variable measurement,
56–59
error, sources of in RtI, 35, 37,
51–56, 61, 63, 140–143
and implementation of RtI, 34, 35
independent variable in RtI,
instruction as, 59, 60
intervention implementation
recommendations, 63–65
positive and negative predictive
power, 47, 48
and professional judgment, 37, 38
questions on, 66

About the Authors

Amanda M. VanDerHeyden, PhD, is a private consultant and researcher whose work has focused on finding practical solutions to problems children face in classrooms. Dr. VanDerHeyden previously has held faculty positions and has worked as a researcher and consultant in a number of school districts. In Vail Unified School District, Dr. VanDerHeyden led a district effort to implement the STEEP Response to Intervention (RtI) model from 2002 to 2005. In this district, identification of children as having specific learning disabilities was reduced by half within 2 years, test scores increased, and the district was nationally recognized as a success story related to No Child Left Behind by the U.S. Department of Education. These data were reported in a journal article that was acclaimed as article of the year by *Journal of School Psychology* in 2007. Dr. VanDerHeyden has authored over 50 related articles and book chapters and has worked as a national trainer and consultant to assist districts to implement RtI models. In 2006, Dr. VanDerHeyden was named to an advisory panel for the National Center for Learning Disabilities to provide guidance related to RtI and the diagnosis of specific learning disability. She is associate editor of *Assessment for Effective Intervention* and serves on the editorial boards for *School Psychology Review, School Psychology Quarterly, Journal of School Psychology, Topics in Early Childhood Special Education, Journal of Early Intervention*, and *Journal of Learning Disabilities*. Dr. VanDerHeyden is coeditor of *The Handbook of Response to Intervention* published by Springer and special issues of *Assessment for Effective Intervention* and *School Psychology Review*, each focusing on RtI. In 2006, Dr. VanDerHeyden received the Lightner Witmer Early Career Contributions Award from Division 16 (School Psychology) of the American Psychological Association in recognition of her scholarship on early intervention, RtI, and models of data-based decision making in schools. She lives with her husband, Chad, and their two young children, Ben and Kate, on the gulf coast in Fairhope, Alabama.

Matthew K. Burns, PhD, is an associate professor of Educational Psychology and coordinator of the School Psychology program at the University of Minnesota. Dr. Burns has published over 100 articles and book chapters in national publications and has coauthored or coedited several books. He is also the editor of *Assessment for Effective Intervention*, the editor elect of *School Psychology Review*, on the editorial board of three other journals, and was a coauthor of *School Psychology: A Blueprint for Training and Practice*. Dr. Burns is a highly sought after speaker regarding response to intervention (RtI), has worked with schools in dozens of states to implement RtI, and has published numerous articles and books about RtI implementation.